Kerry Walks

KERRY WALKS

Updated and Revised

Kerry Walks

Text and illustrations

KEVIN CORCORAN

THE O'BRIEN PRESS
DUBLIN

This revised edition published 2001 by The O'Brien Press Ltd.
20 Victoria Road, Rathgar, Dublin 6, Ireland.
Tel. +353 1 4923333; Fax. +353 1 4922777
E-mail: books@obrien.ie
Website: www.obrien.ie
First published 1992. Revised 1998

ISBN: 0-86278-744-0

British Library Cataloguing in Publication Data
A catalogue record for this book is available from the British Library.

3 4 5 6 7 8 9 10
01 02 03 04 05 06 07 08 09

The O'Brien Press receives
assistance from

Typesetting, design and layout: The O'Brien Press Ltd.
Cover separations: C&A Print Services Ltd.
Printing: Guernsey Press Ltd.

For my father, Danny,
and in memory of my mother, Chrissie

Contents

Introduction 8

Map of Kerry 13

Walks Summary 14

• *Killarney Walks* •

1 Muckross 15

2 The Paps 30

3 Mangerton 38

4 Torc Mountain 40

5 Knockreer 42

6 Old Kenmare Road 44

7 Crohane 46

8 Tomies Wood 48

• *Iveragh Peninsula* •

9 Lough Acoose 51

10 Bray Head 59

11 Lough Currane 66

12 Derrynane 79

13 Rossbeigh 88

• *Dingle* •

14 Anascaul 96

15 Ballydavid Head 106

16 Great Blasket Island 115

17 Mount Eagle 124

18 The Magharees 135

• *Kenmare* •

19 Kenmare Uplands 143

20 Barraboy Ridge 154

Introduction

Kerry, that magical land of mountain and sea, presents the rambler with the ultimate in diversity when it comes to choosing a day's walking. Over three-quarters of the region is mountain, moorland or hilly pasture that either plunges into steep river valleys or plummets over towering sea cliffs. All around, you are exposed to every possible type of glacial feature. From corrie lake to V-shaped valley, ice-cap action to moraine, Kerry has as much to offer as the lofty peaks of the Alps, Northern Scandinavia or even Alaska. These wild mountainous peninsulas, together with the county's position on the western extremity of Europe, have ensured the region's constant exposure to the mild and temperate winds and soft virginal rains of the Atlantic Gulf Stream. Thus its many wild corners throb with a wealth and fascinating collection of wildlife that in places is overwhelming.

As much as a quarter of all rare Irish plants have their headquarters here. Some are endemic to the region, while others belong to different climes though they thrive in the moderate oceanic climate. So, you find American, Mediterranean, Arctic and Alpine plants growing side by side. Some of Kerry's woodlands are several thousand years old and the lushness of the vegetation is at times so rich that it becomes subtropical. Sea birds of both national and international importance breed here, while there is a unique collection of animal life, including native herds of red deer, Ireland's only toad and the Kerry slug.

Sadly, such wild and natural landscapes are becoming harder to find in the overpopulated and heavily industrialised countries of mainland Europe and Britain. There, the silent majority has watched the environment being recklessly sacrificed to the demands of a shortsighted and blinkered view of economic progress. And nature lovers are being increasingly attracted to Ireland in search of what they have lost.

Ironically, this turn of events could now provide a marvellous opportunity for the economy of Ireland. Viewed by many as the Garden of Europe, our environment, if properly protected and developed, could become an asset that no longer speaks of sentiment or aesthetics but of hard cash, jobs and economic growth. But we are slow to learn from the mistakes of others – in fact we seem intent on repeating them. Already, exploitative projects of a few misguided developers, carrying all the hallmarks of instant profit maximisation, are impinging upon some of our most prized locations. Unique sand dunes are being smothered under the blanket of golf courses, many of our more idyllic bays are being plagued with the scourge of tasteless holiday home developments, some of our most picturesque fishing villages are being pushed aside to make room for unsympathetic marina developments and often insensitive interpretative centres are being placed in the most sensitive of areas. To make matters worse, many of these schemes are supported by what can only be described as scandalous planning permissions that illustrate a lack of real understanding of coordinated and long-term development.

Fortunately, a new and better-educated generation is emerging, many of whom have the ideas, the understanding and the foresight to carry through a realistic development of our economy while maintaining a balance with the environment. All they need is a chance to try.

My hope is that by introducing people to the rich heritage of our natural landscape this book may help us proceed towards the future with greater understanding. That is why I decided to write the book, torn as I was between the desire to hide all this beauty away for fear of its destruction or trusting that people would take it to their hearts and guard it jealously. Through these walks I hope to encourage an attitude of protectiveness towards our environment and in so doing give us all a chance to work towards its ultimate preservation for future generations.

MINIMUM IMPACT

Pollution, tourist pressure, litter, habitat destruction and wildlife disturbance are all having a serious impact on the outdoors. How then do we preserve the diminishing natural environment at a time when more and more people want to experience it? How do we reconcile our presence in it at the same time as we try to protect it from us?

Obviously, there is a need for a set of guidelines that will ensure that the effect of the rambler on the environment is one of Minimum Impact.

There is only one basic guideline: Leave the countryside as you yourself would like to encounter it.

Rubbish, whatever its source, is objectionable and we should all help by removing any non-biodegradable litter, such as plastic, aluminium foil, cans and bottles.

Interfering with populations of wild plants and animals is also irresponsible, as many are rare or under threat from diminishing habitats. This is their home. We are merely visitors and should act accordingly.

Many of the wild places are touched by, and even part of, someone else's workplace, especially the farming community. Therefore we should respect both their privacy and their rights and in no way interfere with their property or cause damage to it.

SUITABILITY

These walks have been designed to introduce the walker to our wild and perilously threatened heritage in as safe a manner as possible. They have been categorised into three groups according to their degree of difficulty and the level of fitness required. There is no more miserable way of spending a day than taking on something that is beyond your limits or that you are not suitably equipped to cope with. So check a walk's suitability for your party carefully before setting out. Then you will ensure a good day is had by all.

Casual: These are fairly straightforward walks following well-defined paths and roads. They are suitable for first-time and occasional walkers with young children. None of the more expensive and varied equipment used by regular walkers, such as compasses, waterproof boots or all-weather coats, is necessary. However, sensible clothing is still required. The walks in this category are Nos. 1, 5, 6, 7 (OPTION) 10, 16, 18.

Moderate: These walks involve a certain amount of rough terrain with more taxing demands, such as steep ground or wet conditions. Therefore, they are more suited to those who have already engaged in a certain amount of walking. You would want to be reasonably fit, wear waterproof boots with a good grip and have appropriate clothing. The walks in this category are Nos. 1 (OPTION), 2, 4, 7, 12, 13, 14, 15, 19 (OPTION).

Tough: These walks are really for the more experienced walkers who have a lot of mileage under their belt. They include a lot of very tough terrain that does not always follow an outlined path. Thus you need to be very fit and experienced at coping with awkward conditions. Additionally, you need to carry a compass, have strong waterproof boots and all-weather clothing as well as be able to read maps carefully and accurately and work out a certain amount of facts for yourself in relation to finding your way. The walks in this category are Nos. 3, 8, 9, 11, 14 (OPTION), 17, 19, 20.

THE WALKS

Walking through the various habitats that are found in Kerry, you will come to know the occupants of these diminishing communities, and of their fragile existence and the forces that now threaten them. From woods, mountain, bog, farmland, beach, cliff, dune, to fresh-water lake and river, you can visit them all in different seasons of the year and their significance is illustrated and explained. I have no doubt that they will draw you out again and again to experience the delights of an ever-changing landscape. However, it is not realistic to assume that there will be no danger involved just because these areas have been outlined in the book. It is important to remember a number of points, listed below.

DANGER

Common sense and discretion should always be used when in the wilderness, especially if you are not familiar with the ways of the countryside. Please take note of the following points.

Mountains: The higher peaks are prone to rapidly descending fogs and mists which will make it impossible to descend safely, thus attempt these only on fine clear days when there is no threat of rain and its accompanying low cloud.

Cliffs: These should be treated with the greatest of respect, especially in wet and windy weather when they can be prone to erosion and instant collapse. Keep your distance from them and on no account allow children free reign near them.

Waves: There is such a thing as a freak wave that thunders onto the shore during wild and windy weather. These can turn up irregularly every fifteen to twenty-five minutes, depending on the swell. Most people like to get near the crashing waves on a headland or rock, measuring their safety distance by the waves immediately observed. Tragically, many lives have been lost over the years as unwary visitors have been caught by a sudden and unexpected enormous freak wave.

Rights-of-way: As far as was possible all the routes in this book follow recognised rights-of-way, are across commonages or have been given the blessing of the owner. However, in some cases it was not possible to discern this fully, and land of course may undergo a change of ownership. In general, most landowners are reasonable as long as you respect their property and they are treated with the courtesy they deserve. If difficulties do arise, please be discreet and leave the property promptly but safely (and the author would appreciate the point being brought to his attention).

Poison: On no account should any plants described in this book be tasted or eaten, as many are poisonous and can cause severe if not fatal illness.

Clothing: Wear good boots that have a reasonably good grip. Wet and cold weather can occur at any time of the year, thus you should dress accordingly. It is better to wear several layers of warm clothing than one thick garment, as layers can be taken off and put on depending on conditions. For this purpose it is very handy to have some form of knapsack that leaves your hands free. When doing the tougher walks, a spare pair of shoes and socks is desirable.

USING THE BOOK

Ideally, the text should be read in conjunction with the walk, but it is a good idea to read the entire walk before you set out. Each walk follows a series of numbered points on the accompanying map, with the text at each point providing directions and outlining what to see. Use the map regularly to check your location. Starting at point number one, follow the dotted line onto point number two and so on throughout the route. Note that the end of some walks overlaps the outward route and thus the numbered points reappear in the text. If you lose your bearings at any time, try to find your position on the map and refer to the previous numbered point, which should explain your next move.

WALK DESCRIPTIONS AND CHARACTERISTICS

Distances: All distances are given for the round trip, with the extra distance for the OPTIONS given separately.

Time: This is given as an approximate minimum for the completion of the round trip. Obviously this will vary greatly depending on the people involved and the amount of time they spend stopping and exploring. On average, give yourself half an hour per mile on the casual walks but an hour to the mile for the tough ones, adding on as much time as you like for rests, picnics and so on. In winter be careful of the early sunset and the inevitable darkness which can occur from 16.30 onwards – set out early!

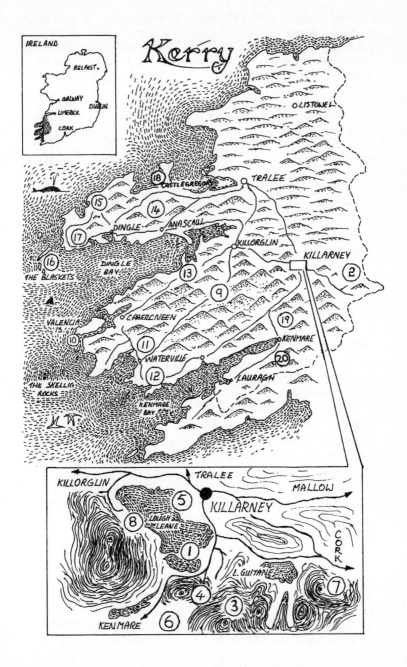

WALKS SUMMARY

WALK	HABITAT	LENGTH	TIME	SUITABILITY
· KILLARNEY ·				
1 Muckross	oak woods	7.5ml/11.5km	4hrs	casual
OPTION		8.5ml/13.1km	5.5hrs	moderate
2 Paps	mountain heath	8ml/13km	5hrs	moderate
3 Mangerton Mt.	upland heath	6ml/10km	5hrs	tough
4 Torc Mt.	woods and heath	5ml/8km	4hrs	moderate
5 Knockreer	demesne, parkland	4ml/6.5km	3hrs	casual
6 Tomies Wood	oak woods	6ml/9.5km	3hrs	casual
7 Old Kenmare Road	mountain heath	10ml/16km	5hrs	moderate
OPTION	oak woods	8ml/12km	4hrs	casual
8 Crohane	mountain heath	4ml/6.5km	4hrs	tough
· IVERAGH ·				
9 Lough Acoose	mountain ridge	5 ml/8km	3hrs	tough
10 Bray Head	coastal island	5ml/8km	3hrs	casual
11 Lough Currane	lake and moor	14ml/22.5km	8hrs	tough
12 Derrynane	coastal beach, heath and woods	5ml/8km	3hrs	moderate
13 Rossbeigh	coastal heath	5ml/8km	4hrs	moderate
· DINGLE ·				
14 Anascaul	mountain peaks	4ml/6.5km	2.5hrs	moderate
OPTION		5.5ml/9km	5hrs	tough
15 Ballydavid	coastal cliffs	5ml/8km	3hrs	moderate
16 Great Blasket	island	4ml/6.5km	5hrs	casual
17 Mount Eagle	coastal mountain	9ml/14.5km	5hrs	tough
18 The Magharees	dunes	5ml/8km	3hrs	casual
· KENMARE ·				
19 Kenmare	mountain heath	8ml/13km	6hrs	tough
OPTION		5ml/8km	3hrs	moderate
20 Barraboy Ridge	mountain	9ml/14.5km	7–8hrs	tough

1 – Muckross

IRELAND, ORIGINALLY AN ISLAND of temperate forest, was once a place where nature reigned supreme. From the end of the last Ice Age, over eight thousand years ago, until relatively recent times, oak forest dominated the landscape. Over five thousand years ago, during Neolithic times, considerable portions of forest began to disappear due to the development of sub-Atlantic bogs and the impact of man. Yet, by the end of the sixteenth century over one-eighth of the country was still heavily forested, mainly in the steep river valleys and mountainous regions.

It was only in the more recent past that any significant change occurred, a change that transformed the appearance of the island beyond recognition, decimating the remaining bulk of its ancient woodlands. During the sixteenth century, the conquest and subsequent colonisation of Ireland was in full swing. Amidst the ensuing slaughter, it was in the ancient woods that the displaced Irish took refuge from the invading armies. Thus to the conqueror, the forests were often seen as a major obstacle to total colonisation and would therefore have to go. *A Discourse of Ireland* of 1601 stated that 'the woods and bogs are a great hindrance to us and help to the rebels, who can, with a few men, kill as many of ours … It would have been a better course to have burnt down all the woods.' They were also seen as a vast untapped resource by the new overlords of the

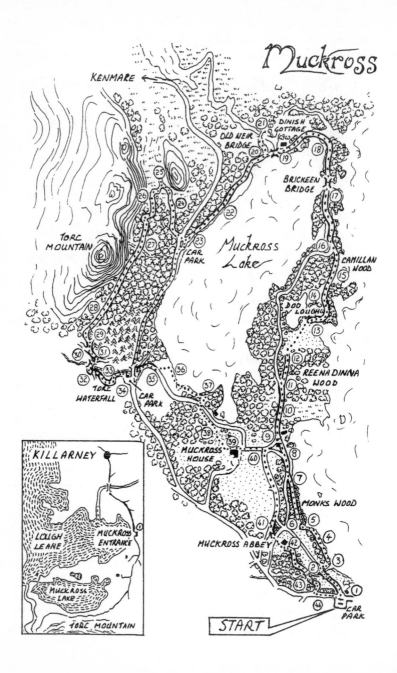

seventeenth century. And so they became the source of raw materials for shipbuilding, tanning of leather, pipe and barrel-stave making and iron smelting. Within a short time, the principal ruling settlers had set up their mills and their wood-burning furnaces for the smelting of iron, fed upon the ancient oaks.

'In the east-west valleys of Cork and Kerry lay mile after mile of forests which were to enrich the Boyles, the Pettys, the Whites and for a short but intensive period, Sir Walter Raleigh; forests which in the first part of the seventeenth century were to cask nearly all the wine that France and a great deal of Spain would produce; which would float as the hulls of many of the East India Company's ships; which until the mid-eighteenth century would fill the insatiable furnaces of the ironworks that lined the river valleys and which would provide the bark for the tanneries of Killarney ...' By the end of the eighteenth century the woods were all but gone and the ancient once-forested kingdom had been utterly changed for all time.

It is hard to imagine today what a wondrous country Ireland must have originally been. Thus, it is a great delight to learn that a tiny fraction of this forest system has survived where one can experience to some small degree the glories of the past. This priceless gem of our most ancient heritage sits amidst the foothills of the country's highest mountain, Carrauntoohil, around the lakes and glens of Killarney, and is probably one of the loveliest parts of Ireland if not Western Europe.

WALK DESCRIPTION

LOCATION: Within Killarney's National Park, 2ml/3km from the nearby town. Take the Kenmare road and park at the car park opposite the jaunting-car entrance to Muckross Demesne.

TERRAIN: A casual circular walk through the ancient woods that circle the lakes and cloak the mountains. Following the paths and roadways that weave about Killarney's National Park, it is a walk that is suitable for all. There is also an OPTION available along a tough and spectacular path that gives magnificent views over the entire park.

FEATURES: Native oak forest and its abundant wildlife; Muckross Demesne with its fifteenth-century abbey and nineteenth-century Elizabethan Revival manor house; Killarney lakes; Dinish Island; the Meeting of the Waters and the Old Weir Bridge; Torc Waterfall; rare plants and animals.

LENGTH: 7.5ml/11.5km. OPTION: 1ml/1.6km extra.

TIME: 4hrs. OPTION: 1.5hrs extra.

EQUIPMENT: Comfortable walking shoes. The OPTION requires strong boots.

WHEN TO WALK: Enjoyable at any time of the year, but since it is a prime tourist spot the area can be quite congested during mid-summer and bank holiday weekends.

WALK OUTLINE

(1) On arriving at the main entrance to Muckross Demesne, park in the car park opposite. This is usually surrounded by a clutter of horse-drawn jaunting cars. Cross the road and pass through the limestone pillared gates, following the avenue that leads to the main house.

Beyond the picturesque lodge entrance, stunning vistas of the charming lakes and their impressive mountain backdrop unfold before you. It is a scene that is extensively photographed and a fitting introduction to the wonders that lie ahead.

(2) The avenue soon passes over a bridge. Cross it and turn to the RIGHT immediately. Walk through the meadow and beside the river towards the trees and follow the woodland path down to the lakeshore.

The bridge is adorned with decorative wrought-iron railings, its carved, limestone pillars having the letters H.A.H. and the year 1878 inscribed on them. These are the initials of Henry Arthur Herbert, who built the manor house in 1843. Thus the bridge must be a later addition, erected during the embellishment of the estate. The woods that lead down to the shoreline are mixed, incorporating SYCAMORE, ASH and SCOTS PINE. However, these are not part of the ancient forest system, being nothing more than a collection of trees that were set as part of the estate's landscaping. They have now become wild and support a healthy variety of wild flowers and regenerating tree seedlings.

(3) On reaching the lake, turn to the LEFT and walk along the rough and awkward, though natural, stonecobbled shoreline.

Across the waters, the tree-smothered slopes of Tomies Wood merge into blankets of heath that stretch smoothly upwards towards the peaks of Shehy and Tomies mountains. Out on the lake, small tree-canopied islands of white limestone rock contrast sharply with the old red sandstone of the surrounding mountains. This curious abutting of the lowland's alkaline soil on the acid of old red sandstone mountains is one of the features of Killarney's wonders, conferring on the area a unique geological composition and a resultant mix of plant and animal life that is unrivalled throughout the country.

(4) As you walk along the wave-rippled shore, a screen of water-loving ALDER trees guards your left side. Beneath them and pouring out onto the path are rich clumps of PURPLE LOOSESTRIFE (*Lythrum salicaria*),

SNEEZEWORT (*Achillea ptarmica*) and the heavily scented WATER MINT (*Mentha aquatica*), all of which are in flower during late summer. Earlier in the year, you should find the yellow blobs of MARSH MARIGOLD (*Caltha palustris*) by the water's edge.

(5) When the shoreline comes to an end near some limestone cliffs, the route swings into the trees on the LEFT, and then takes a sharp RIGHT along an earth path towards an old stone wall.

(6) When you reach the wall, keep it to your left, climb the few stone steps and towards the other end pass through the break in the wall. This leads you into Monk's Wood, a delightful woodland glade through which a romantic path guides you STRAIGHT ahead.

Sneezewort produces its tall stand of white blossoms in August, wherever there is damp ground.

Giant OAKS and BEECH tower above your head, while thick swards of the coarse GREATER WOODRUSH (*Luzula sylvatica*) border the path on either side. Numerous birds move about the trees, ranging from the small BLUE TITS to the larger but more elusive JAYS. Across the woodland floor, there is a constant flutter of SPECKLED WOOD BUTTERFLIES, caught beneath the spotlight of beams that break through the thick canopy of leaves on sun-filled summer days.

(7) When the path emerges onto the tarred road, go to the RIGHT towards Muckross House.

Presently the magnificent manor house comes into view across the sweeping parkland on the left. Thickly surrounded by specimen trees, the building exudes an air of romantic grandeur and wealth from the Victorian age. Its gabled roofs and towering chimneys peep through the trees of its fairytale setting.

(8) Shortly a Y-junction is reached with a sign for Dinish Cottage and the Meeting of the Waters, 2.3ml/3.7km. Take the RIGHT branch here.

This leads you through some shady woods, which support rich growths of HART'S TONGUE FERN (*Asplenium scolopendrium*) and WINTER HELIOTROPE (*Petasites fragans*). Later, you pass a picturesque stone boathouse on the right and arrive at another Y-junction, flanked by a pretty stone cottage.

(9) At this second Y-junction go to the RIGHT and follow the tarred road

Many dragonflies that emerge from the lakes will have their 'hunting beats' over the surrounding vegetation. This ashnea dragonfly is our biggest and most powerful predatory insect.

that leads you on to Reenadinna Wood.

In the centre of the junction's grassy island is a large CANADIAN MAPLE tree. This tree is spectacular in its autumn colours, turning an incredible golden yellow in late October. Just beyond the Y-junction on your right is Arthur Vincent House.

(10) On rounding the next bend the trees give way to an open boggy tract, full of HEMP AGRIMONY (*Eupatorium cannabinum*). This grows quite tall and produces an abundance of pale pink flowerheads in the late summer. These draw large numbers of butterflies on warm sunny days and there should be plenty of SILVER WASHED FRITILLARY and PEACOCK on offer. You may also spot a variety of dragonflies in summer.

(11) After 0.25ml/0.4km you arrive at a path branching off to the RIGHT at a Y-junction. Nearby is a stone marker with an arrow, ignore this and follow the path up into the trees of Reenadinna Wood.

As you walk beneath the canopy of trees, you may notice that they are of a different type to the wooded roadsides left behind. This is a rather unique wood of YEW trees (*Taxus baccata*) which grows here remarkably well, pushing up through the bedrock of bare limestone. The woodland floor is covered in an extraordinary carpet of mossy tufts. These give a surreal effect, being the only plant that can grow substantially in the dark shade cast by the evergreen yew. In the late autumn or winter, these trees are alive with flocks of FIELDFARES (*Turdus pilaris*) gorging themselves on the red fruits of the yew. These thrush-like birds migrate to Ireland from Scandinavia each winter.

(12) The YEW woods open out into fine old meadowland. Walk out along the path then turn RIGHT to cross the meadows.

All around, the field borders are dressed in the luxuriant foliage of numerous old OAKS, their lower trunks surrounded by thickets of wild flowers. During the summer months, these old hay meadows of the estate farm are allowed to grow their rich crops of hay. These become filled with wild herbs and flowers which in turn support many insects and caterpillars. They are reminiscent of earlier days when farming was less intensive and allowed humans to live in harmony with nature. The disappearance of old meadows has been one of the main causes of the rapid decline of that unusual and now seldom-heard bird, the CORNCRAKE (*Crex crex*). These summer visitors to our shores are totally dependent on the hay meadow as a nesting site.

(13) Having crossed the field diagonally, you reach the OAK woods again. Here follow the old track through the gap and into the trees of Camillan Wood.

This is an excellent example of the native oak woods. Fine old SESSILE OAKS (*Quercus petraea*) dominate the tree layer while the underlying shrubs are mostly evergreens like HOLLY, YEW and ARBUTUS. The ground flora is sparse with large thickets of WOODRUSH, FROTHEN, WOOD SORREL and FERN being predominant. However, along with the evergreens, it is the rich growth of plants on the trees that makes these woods so special. Vast amounts of MOSSES, LIVERWORTS, FILMY FERNS and LICHEN coat the trees, thriving in the moist oceanic climate of Killarney.

(14) A swampy tract is reached in which the trees change to ALDER and ASH. On the ground beneath them, tall stands of reeds hide the watery mire. Listen for bird song in the canopy above, where BLUE TITS and FINCH flit about the branches in search of insects hiding in the thick coating of LICHENS. During hot summer evenings, if you listen very carefully, you can hear the deep drone of the HOVER FLIES and BEES which frequent the cooler shade of the tree tops.

(15) Further on, the mature OAK woods return. Sadly, they have been invaded by the suffocating scourge of RHODODENDRON. Introduced to Ireland in the nineteenth century from the warmer climes of Turkey and Portugal, they have adapted only too well to the generally frost-free climate of Killarney. As an introduced species, the rhododendron grows unchecked, unable to fit in with the ecological balance of the native forest. It now threatens the entire forest system, as it smothers all ground life beneath its thick tangle of branches and impenetrable shade. The final death will come when, through the absence of seed regeneration, no more oaks grow to replace the present generation of adult trees. Frustratingly, we must accept the fact that we have set in motion the death sentence of this unique heirloom.

Despite the valiant attempts of young voluntary groups like Groundwork and the park wardens to eradicate this alien, rhododendron shoots emerge quickly from the coppiced stools or germinate from seed. I can never resist pulling a few new shoots of these irritating plants each

Arbutus – the red fruits of this unusual tree ripen in winter.

time I pass. A futile attempt to suppress their onslaught, but then again if everyone of you who passed…!

(16) When the lane eventually joins the tarred road again, go to the RIGHT.

Soon the waters of Muckross Lake are seen through the trees on the left, with Torc Mountain as a backdrop. From here on, watch the foliage of the overhead trees. Numerous STRAWBERRY or ARBUTUS trees grow here, curious evergreens, whose characteristic red berries appear in the winter. They are more familiar with the shores of the Mediterranean than of Killarney, and are of that unusual group of Lusitanian plants that are unique to Ireland's south-west. Believed to date from the end of the last Ice Age when the forests first appeared, they are a stamp of identity for the ancient forest system. However, no one knows for certain how they came to be in Ireland.

(17) Presently the Brickeen Bridge is met, its unusual Gothic arch spanning the meeting of Muckross Lake and Lough Leane. To your right the fine old OAKS of Tomies Wood run up the sides of Shehy Mountain. If it weren't for their total infestation by the stifling RHODODENDRON, this would probably be the most unique and perfect example of aboriginal forest in the entire country. Looking out across the other side of the bridge, Torc Mountain rises up from the shoreline of the lake, its lower slopes also covered in thick forest. There too, from the month of May onwards, the deep infestation of rhododendron becomes only too obvious as masses of pink blossoms cover the wooded hillside.

(18) Continuing along the tarred road, delightful woodland glades open periodically to give memorable views of wooded mountain slopes, across reed-fringed lakes. At any time of the year, the woodland paradise of these lakes and mountains has a limitless magic. Whether it be during the first blooming of the spring trees or during the bursts of autumn colours across the heathery glens, each visit is as memorable as the first.

(19) On arriving at Dinish Cottage, you have passed unknowingly on to

Dinish Island. The cottage is surrounded with an interesting collection of ornamental plants sat in the last century. These include EUCALYPTUS, CALIFORNIAN REDWOODS, AZALEAS, MAGNOLIAS, CAMELLIAS and other rare tropical plants. Refreshments are available here and there is no more delightful place to take a break than by the Meeting of the Waters at the rear of the cottage gardens. This looks across a deep swirling pool, surrounded by bowing old OAKS, towards the romantic Old Weir Bridge. Keep an eye open for KINGFISHERS, small diving birds that skim the water-top in an eye-blink of luminous blue and orange.

(20) Leaving the cottage behind, cross a small bridge and watch for a worn path going into the trees on the RIGHT. From here, you can take a short detour to see the Old Weir Bridge but you will have to return again to the tarred road to complete the walk. If you wish to skip the detour, proceed along the road to (22).

(21) Some way ahead, you may spot a small marker pole with its top painted red. Walk towards this and continue through the rough rhododendron-cleared woodland, towards the Old Weir Bridge. This is a delightful rustic stone bridge. After rain the rapids pour violently under its double arch and it is a bit hair-raising to watch the long boats negotiate them. These large rowing boats are used to ferry tourists from the Gap of Dunloe back through the lakes to Ross Castle. One capsized in 1938 and several people were drowned. On returning to the tarred road, resume your journey by going to the RIGHT.

(22) The road leads you again through more delightful stretches of woodland, full of SCOTS PINE and OAK. Amongst the oak leaf foliage, a rare butterfly can sometimes be encountered. This is the PURPLE HAIRSTREAK (*Quercusia quercus*), one of our scarcest Irish butterflies. Although the male is a spectacular purple colour, it inhabits the upper oak canopy and may be hard to spot. Additionally, its larvae are disguised to look like an oak bud and therefore evade detection.

The purple hairstreak is recognised by the purple streaks on the wings of the male and by its close association with the oak tree.

The Old Weir Bridge arches over the rapids that exit from the Upper Lake. Boats travel down the rapids under this bridge.

(23) The avenue eventually arrives at an open car park, alongside the main Killarney-Kenmare road.

The OPTION becomes available here. If you wish TO SKIP THE OPTION enter the car park, go to the LEFT and walk with extreme care back along the very busy main road to Torc Waterfall. Rejoin the walk at (34).

OPTION

This is a very tough and at times taxing trek that follows a rough footpath up the wooded slopes of Torc Mountain. It involves clambering over rocks and much stooping. It is not suitable for the unfit or for very small children. You climb almost to the top of the mountain in front of you, just above the tree line of conifers. Be warned it is tough.

On arriving at the car park, go out by the RIGHT-HAND exit. Cross the busy main road carefully and enter the small picnic area on the other side. At the top of the stepped slope join the path.

Worn and torn, it climbs steeply through dense thickets of RHODODENDRON. From this entangling shrubbery, tall and lanky EUCALYPTUS trees protrude from amongst the more native OAKS and YEWS.

(24) The trees finally give way to open heath. Smothered in thickets of HEATHER and FURZE, it is awash with a sea of purple and yellow in August. Behind you, fine vistas of the lakeland walk unfold, while above your head, RAVENS croak-call from the cliffed rim of Torc Mountain.

(25) The path begins to level out at the top and eventually takes a sharp turn to the LEFT at a fork in the path. But first go STRAIGHT ahead to take advantage of the marvellous views into the distant mountains that surround the most beautiful of all the lakes.

A less distinct path leads forward to a small rock. Below, the magnificent and sparkling waters of the Long Range and the more distant Upper Lake snake away from you, their surrounding hills draped in lush OAK forest. During October, the male RED DEER, or stags, bellow across the glens in their traditional rutting call. The Killarney herd of native red deer is a special feature of the park, being the last remaining herd of pure Irish descent. In all, it contains only several hundred deer and is the remnants of the great wild herds that used to roam the forests in ancient times. Return to the bend in the path, and go to the RIGHT.

(26) The path enters the rocky woods, scrambling over boulders and turf banks. Though this makes progress somewhat arduous, the path should be discernible at all times. Walking below the cliffed skyline and out above the wood, you see the panoramic views of Muckross Lake and Lough Leane spread out below, with the outline of Ross Castle in the middle distance and, further away, the town of Killarney.

(27) The path eventually leads back into the RHODODENDRONS and DESCENDS a very steep and rough incline. Some steps help the descent, but caution still needs to be exercised. Later, the path crosses a stream which can be awkward when in winter flood, but is still traversable with a little care.

Along the stream's edge are clumps of the rarer KIDNEY SAXIFRAGE (*Saxifraga hirsuta*), a close cousin to ST PATRICK'S CABBAGE (*Saxifraga spatularis*). These are members of the unique Lusitanian group, characteristic of the West Cork and Kerry mountains. Such spots used to be the home of the now extremely rare KILLARNEY FERN (*Trichomanes speciosum*). The future of this plant is uncertain due to the short-sighted gathering habits of nineteenth-century Victorian collectors, which left no sustainable populations of the plant to reproduce!

(28) Continue through the tunnel of RHODODENDRON thickets on your RIGHT to arrive at an open space. This has a picnic table and a vista point looking down on the neighbouring demesne of Muckross House. Further down the path, you will come across a well and a stone gazebo, built under a rock. These are remnants from the earlier days of the estate, when numerous paths snaked about the woodlands to delight the gentry.

(29) The path leads DOWN into a coniferous plantation. Passing through this, the path opens onto a clearing where it meets a rough track. Swing to the RIGHT here and follow the track down through the state-planted pine woods.

(30) When you arrive at a T-junction, go to the LEFT for 82ft/25m. As you walk, you hear the rumbles of a mountain river below on the right and soon you come to a bend. STOP.

(31) At the bend leave the track and turn into the RIGHT. A steep path descends to the Owengarriff river where a stone bridge crosses a number of small pools and falls.

(32) At the other side of the bridge, a stile leads onto the path again. This you continue to follow, taking the first LEFT branch that leads down the wooded slope towards Torc Waterfall.

Exposed roots of the surrounding trees trail across the well-worn path, a sign of the effects excessive tourist pressure can have on the environment. Our very presence in the countryside has a cumulative effect, which if not controlled wreaks havoc on the fragile ecosystem. We must therefore accept responsibility for our own actions and take all necessary precautions to minimise our presence, whether by simply taking home all our litter or by not exploiting any part of the wilderness as a cheap commercial product. Such a fear has been expressed for the whole of Killarney's National Park, where the idea of cable cars running up the side of Torc Mountain has been mooted. Already, the out-of-place water buses ferry tourists up and down the lake, despite the pleas of environmentally aware groups for cautious economic development of the park. Such over-exploitation of the park will sound the death knell for Killarney as surely as the rhododendrons do for its woods.

(33) Torc Waterfall cascades down the mossy green slopes of the steep ravine, foaming white against its sheltering mantle of greenery. It makes a romantic picture and one which is best seen during the late autumn. Then, the first floods pour over the edge in fountains of sparkling spray, the surrounding trees are a riot of autumn copper reds, yellows and browns and, of course, there are fewer tourists.

(34) Leaving the waterfall behind, continue DOWN the path to the car park. Pass the small building, keeping it on your right, and walk STRAIGHT ahead to pass underneath the road by means of the tunnel by the river. This brings you back into Muckross Demesne, where you rejoin the tarred avenue and go to the LEFT, following the sign for Muckross House and Gardens.

(35) Come out from beneath the canopy of trees and the open parkland stretches before you down to the shore of Muckross Lake. Leaving the avenue, walk towards the shoreline on your LEFT. (NOTE: Avoid in winter due to floods and proceed to point (38) by staying on the avenue.)

(36) At the water's edge, swing to the RIGHT and walk towards the trees which are visible in the distance. The waters of the lake are empty of birdlife because the lake is deep and does not provide the type of feeding for a lot of the more common duck. However, the lake is rich in fish life and its associated insect food. So you will encounter DRAGON and DAMSELFLIES throughout the summer, as well as numerous displays of CADDIS and MAYFLIES from the spring onwards.

(37) When you reach a stretch of sandy beach backed with SCOTS PINE, take the path on the RIGHT going under the trees. Follow this onto a tarred road, and then go to the LEFT.

(38) Take the signposted path on the RIGHT for the gardens of Muckross House.

As you make your way up to the main house, the path wanders through a magnificent display of ornamental shrubs and flower beds. Mature stands of woodland trees and flowering RHODODENDRONS of every possible hue run in an informal maze across the wide expanses of manicured lawn. Basking in semi-tropical conditions, plants from all corners of the world dazzle and amaze the eye. GIANT REDWOODS and MONTEREY PINE from the Californian coast, AZALEAS and CABBAGE TREES from New Zealand, TREE FERNS from the Azores, MONKEY PUZZLES from Chile, MAGNOLIAS from the Himalayas and CEDARS from Japan, are all to be found scattered throughout the garden.

(39) On arriving at the house, walk past its creeper-clad walls and large windows to reach the front entrance.

This splendid Elizabethan Revival mansion, with its enchanting views of the surrounding lakes and mountains, never fails to impress. Built between the years 1839 and 1843 by Col. H. A. Herbert to the designs of the Scottish architect William Burns, it has sixty-two chimneys and twenty-five bedrooms and cost £30,000. The towering chimneys amid the pointed finials of its stepped gables, its rich tracery of mullioned windows and majestic oriels draped in VIRGINIA CREEPER, all combine to create the perfect setting for any Elizabethan romance. It has attracted many distinguished visitors over the years – including Queen Victoria and Prince Albert with their hundred-strong retinue in the year 1861, Edward VII, Empress Eugenie of France, George Bernard Shaw and William Butler

Muckross Abbey lends a peaceful tranquility to the surrounding parkland.

Yeats. In 1899 the estate passed into the hands of the Guinness family through Lord Ardilaun, who sold it before the outbreak of World War I to a wealthy American, Bowers Bourne. He gave it as a wedding present to his daughter Maud on her marriage to the American senator Arthur Vincent. When Maud died at a tragically young age, Vincent, along with his parents-in-law, left the entire park to the Irish people in 1932. Vincent conveys the spirit in which he intended the estate to be developed: 'I want especially to have the young people come to Muckross to trail those mountains and to enjoy nature in all its aspects. I hope that Muckross will be made a real garden of friendship...'

(40) Leaving Muckross House behind you, walk STRAIGHT down the main entrance avenue and take the first RIGHT turn with a signpost for Jaunting Car Exit. Continue along this avenue, keeping STRAIGHT until you reach the top of the hill.

As you cross the wide open farmland, a herd of black cattle may be seen. These are pedigree KERRY CATTLE, dating back to the Stone Age, which were at one time the dominant Irish breed. Even though they are well suited to severe weather conditions and the poor pastures of the mountains, they are now confined to the estate and retained by the Irish state on behalf of the nation.

(41) A signpost for Muckross Abbey and Friars' Walk stands at the top of the hill, pointing down to the LEFT. Follow the track DOWN through the spectacular avenue of towering CHESTNUT and LIME trees to arrive at a tarred avenue. Cross this and keep STRAIGHT on for the abbey, partially visible in the trees ahead.

The abbey was founded in 1448 by Donal MacCarthy Mór as a Franciscan friary. Like many Irish abbeys it has a chequered history of plunder, torture and pillage. On a more romantic note, it was the fairytale setting for the midnight marriage of the sixteenth-century heiress to the Muckross estates. In 1588, the young Lady Ellen MacCarthy Mór foiled the attempts of the Crown to gain control of her lands through a proposed marriage to Sir Nicholas Brown. Instead, it is told, she secretly sailed across the lake by moonlight to marry her cousin Florence MacCarthy Reagh, who, for thwarting the Crown, subsequently spent the rest of his life in the Tower of London. However, the lands of Muckross remained in the family.

(42) Having explored the abbey, go to the outer, north rear corner of the building (on the right as you entered the abbey), pass through two separate arches, down some steps and follow the muddy path to the LEFT.

(43) Continuing along the path, cross over a small bridge and through a stile into some BEECH woods. Here, the path goes up to the LEFT and then weaves to the RIGHT through the trees to emerge onto a footpath alongside the main road.

(44) At the roadside, go 328ft/100m to the LEFT to reach the walk's end and your parked car.

2 – The Paps

SCATTERED ACROSS THE CELTIC WORLD are many stone artifacts of great age, their raw material allowing them to survive the test of time. But no written materials survive concerning their origins, leaving the chronicles of the ancient stone builders subject to conjecture, fable and theory. A mix of fact and legend about these early races and their deeds has been passed down by word of mouth from generation to generation.

One such legendary race was the Tuatha Dé Danann, the people of the goddess Dana, who occupied Ireland from about 1500 BC. The Tuatha Dé Danann were believed to have great magical powers. However, with time their powers faded, and they were eventually defeated by the invading Milesians and driven beneath the hills and raths of the countryside to become the fairies of modern Irish folklore. Credited with building the great sepulchral monument of Newgrange, they left behind them numerous other artifacts and many placenames connected with their pagan gods. Kerry is no exception, having a magical pair of mountain peaks called after their supreme deity – the Paps of Dana or, in Gaelic, *Dhá Choich Dhana* (the two breasts of Dana).

The gods of the Tuatha Dé Danann continued to be worshipped by the Gaels up to the fifth century AD, when Christian monks tried to eradicate pagan worship, substituting Christian rites and rituals in place of pagan ones by renaming their gods. Today, Christian religious rituals continue in many ancient pagan sites, such as the May Day celebration of the Blessed Virgin in 'the City' or former shrine to Dana at the foot of the Paps.

So, welcome to the Paps, the ancient pagan land of the mother of the gods, Dana, where atop the two perfectly rounded hills or 'breasts' of Dana stand the timeworn burial mounds of her followers. The Paps are still a place of pilgrimage, but now amongst those who want to gaze upon the rugged wilderness of its rolling heaths and touch the pulse of the true earth.

WALK DESCRIPTION

LOCATION: The Paps are part of the Derrynasaggart mountain range, where the western extremity of Kerry borders with county Cork. The walk starts 13ml/21km from Killarney town. Taking the N22 to Cork, watch for and take the signposted road on the LEFT to 'Clonkeen Church and Clydagh Valley', which is a mile or so after the main turn-off for Kenmare. Having travelled a few metres down the Clonkeen road, take the small side road that branches off to the RIGHT, signposted the 'Clydagh River Valley'. Travel along this side road for about 2.5ml/4km and watch for a track branching off to the LEFT; this leads up into a narrow valley and has a few buildings at its start. Parking is possible at the bottom of the track.

TERRAIN: A moderate circular walk that follows a steep climb up and over the Paps, then crosses the expansive tracts of heath to return by way of delightful back roads and little-used mountain tracks. This is a tough, steep climb (2284ft/760m), the initial part being very wet and more suited to the experienced and fit.

OPTION: A short cut is available after point (13), which connects to point (16). See NOTE at end of first paragraph of point (13). This is part of the 'Duhallow Way Trail', and is clearly marked on OS map No. 79.

FEATURES: The Paps mountains with their uninterrupted scenic views into Cork and Kerry; mountain-top cairns; impressive expanses of heather-clad bog; stone fort; green-roads; mountain lake.

LENGTH: 8ml/13km. OPTION: 6ml/10km.

TIME: 5hrs. OPTION: 4hrs.

EQUIPMENT: Comfortable walking boots with a change of softer walking shoes for the quiet country roads. On the exposed hilltops you may require a windproof jacket.

WHEN TO WALK: Suitable at any time of the year but should not be attempted when low mist or clouds cover the peaks. Late August and September are good months to catch the riotous blooming of the heather.

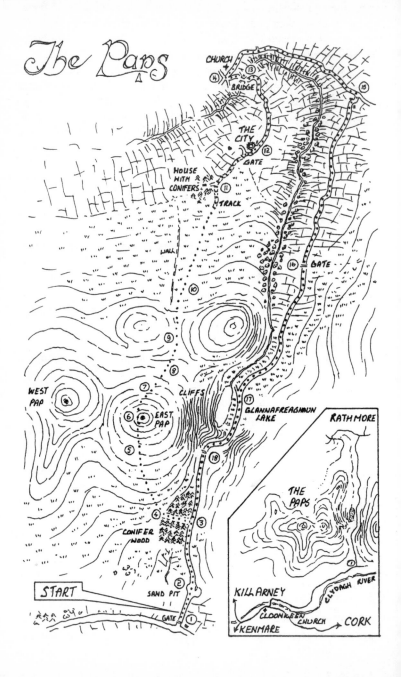

The Paps

WALK OUTLINE

(1) Arriving at the start of the old track, pass through the gate (reclose it).

This old route over the mountains connected the remote rural communities of this, the Clydagh river valley, with the small town of Rathmore on the other side of the mountain. Rising up through a rocky cleft in the mountains, the route passes through the boggy heaths and moors that surround the mountain lake on the other side. This terrain is possibly reflected in the route's old name, *An Sloigeadal*, which in Irish means 'a boggy quagmire'. Many of the former bogs were treacherous places with deep pools of SPHAGNUM MOSS and water that could suck a person under very quickly. With the advent of drainage, most of these bogs have now vanished.

(2) The track continues on STRAIGHT passing through a second gate (reclose). Ahead, a coniferous wood, presently being clear felled, covers the lower slopes, above which the flat, smooth heath of the Paps runs up on your left. It is through these trees the climb to the summit begins.

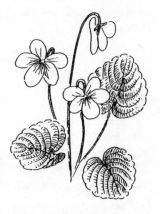

Walking up the stony track, you can see several grasses and small wild flowers growing about the margins. They can survive more successfully here than on the open heath where they must compete with the tall grasses. Watch for TORMENTIL (*Potentilla erecta*), HEATH MILKWORT (*Polygala serpyllifolia*), and EYEBRIGHT (*Euphrasia arctica*), while in the wetter patches the BOG VIOLET (*Viola palustris*), distinguished from other violets by its larger leaves, displays its pale lilac flowers in the early days of summer.

The bog violet grows in damp places, preferring the water-logged soils of boggy heaths to the drier hedge banks colonised by the dog violet.

(3) On passing through a third gate, take the adjacent fire break opening through the conifers, on your LEFT. Some wire fencing may block the way, but climb over it and follow the very wet, open passage to the very top.

Though rocky and smothered in sheaves of MOOR GRASS, a well-trodden path leads you upwards through the conifers. A few birds exploit the temporary shelter of these trees, mainly songbirds like FINCH and TIT.

(4) On breaking out of the trees, go at an angle to the RIGHT across the waves of heather and make for the top.

The tall scrub of PURPLE HEATHER (*Erica cinerea*) lower down can be a bit hard to negotiate so take your time, resting occasionally, as it is a very steep uphill slog. On the way up, you may pass a number of small circular stone clusters, probably the remains of very ancient dwellings, whose age is exceedingly hard to determine without some form of proper excavation.

(5) As you near the top, progress is easier because the heather is dwarfed at the higher and more exposed altitude. The heath comes into its glorious autumnal bloom of pinks and purples in August and September, eclipsing the flush of yellow from the native DWARF GORSE (*Ulex gallii*). Numerous tiny moths are visible about the heath in July and August. You may spot the big brown caterpillars of the OAK EGGAR MOTH (*Lasiocampa quercus*), a favourite food of the migrant CUCKOOS which arrive each summer.

(6) On reaching the summit, survey the view. Then climb down the other side by going at a slight angle to your RIGHT. Be wary of the dangerous cliffs on the extreme right.

The summit of this, the eastern Pap, is crowned by a fine stone mound or cairn. This, when seen from the lowlands, forms one of the characteristic 'nipples' of the breasts of Dana – there is a corresponding 'nipple' or cairn on the western Pap. These stone cairns are probably burial mounds to the high priests/priestesses or the chieftains of the Tuatha Dé Danann. They are approximately 3500 years old and, sadly, are beginning to show their considerable age. Depressingly, sightseers visiting the peak clamber recklessly over the cairn or rip stones from it in order to write their names across the mountain summit. Possibly unaware of how old and significant this monument is, they are wreaking havoc on the structure.

(7) Leaving the cairn behind you, continue to DESCEND the steep, smooth slopes of HEATHER, making for the dip in the hill.

Ahead of you is the flat and broad expanse of lowland bog and fertile farmland that comprises north Cork and south Tipperary, a very different landscape from the one you have left behind. Some small rocky outcrops are clustered near the top, affording some shelter from the cutting winds that blow across the exposed mountain peak. If you look between their shattered stones, you will discover a few species like stunted BUCKLER FERN and ST PATRICK'S CABBAGE (*Saxifraga*

The large black slug is still safe from predators despite the absence of a shell. Covered in slime, when threatened it contracts into a distasteful gelatinous blob.

spatularis). Other hardy plants that thrive this high up are the ground-hugging growths of LICHEN. These grey-green plants can feed almost exclusively on air, extracting the necessary minerals they need from air-borne particles. Slow-growing, they shelter amidst the mosses and stunted heather and are capable of surviving in the most extreme conditions. Occasionally you may spot the large BLACK SLUGS (*Arion ater*) which feed on this impoverished vegetation. As these snails do not have shells, they do not require minerals such as calcium, thus they can survive extremely well in the mineral-deficient soils of the upland, at times reproducing to almost plague proportions.

(8) Coming DOWN towards the first rise, you should be able to see some of the cliffed eastern side of this Pap on your right, with the old road coursing its way up the valley below.

Above the road, a rich mosaic of brown-gold bracken, green-yellowed heath and grey-white splattered stone scree runs up the side of Knocknabro, with the rounded brow of Caherbarnagh beyond it. These form a series of rounded heather-clad hills that provide the type of open terrain necessary for birds, such as GROUSE, which feed almost exclusively on young heather shoots – no heather, no grouse.

(9) On coming OVER the first rise in the hill, the lower expanse of flat heath is visible below you. Some turf-cutting is taking place and you should also see a long stone wall running straight across the flat bog. Looking at an angle to your RIGHT, find a small grove of conifers around a house where the edge of the bog meets the green fields (11). A lane runs out of the bog here – head for this (north by northeast).

(10) Coming DOWN onto the flatter bog, you see the HEATHER develop into an impressive thick sward that is full of insect life. One group of prime feeders in these habitats is the SPIDER, which you can recognise from its web, especially when it glistens with dew drops on a frosty morning. The orb web, made by the GARDEN CROSS SPIDER (*Araneidae*), consists of a large circular disc that is usually stretched across a path or between plants. Hammock webs are made by MONEY SPIDERS (*Linyphia triangularis*), and these are draped across vegetation to hang down just like a hammock.

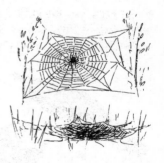

The orb web (top) can be quite large with a width of 2 ft/0.7m, while the hammock web (below) is much smaller. However, both are effective and deadly traps for the insects of the moor.

(11) Once on the lane, follow it as it swings RIGHT. It becomes a better and more solid track as it nears the green fields. Turn around to catch the fine views up to the Paps.

(12) The lane leads you DOWN to a gate, pass through (please reclose), and come out onto a Y-junction. Go to the RIGHT, and follow the tarred road.

Just beyond this junction and on the left-hand side of the road, is an unassuming stone fort. Around it are gathered a few sheds and low cottages, and within is a conspicuous statue of the Blessed Virgin. You have now arrived at the Cathair or 'the City', which is supposed to have been lived in by a sisterhood of maidens who worshipped the goddess Dana during the late Bronze Age. However, with the arrival of Christianity, the fort eventually became a penitential station.

During the earlier part of this century, the feast of the Blessed Virgin was celebrated with great gusto on May Day. The Catholic faithful came in great numbers to carry out the traditional rounds, circling the stone enclosure, while reciting prayers and inscribing crosses on the most prominent stones. Many tents would be erected within the stone perimeter, selling wares from sweets to trinkets. However, the sellers pulled many of the stones from the walls to anchor their canvas tents against the wind, while many more stones were carted further afield to erect new buildings. As a result, the fort is now in a serious state of decay.

One stone house remains within the City confines, however, and this was lived in until quite recently, which makes it the longest-inhabited ring fort in the western world – from the Bronze Age, over 3500 years ago, up to the twentieth century!

(13) Leaving the City, follow the tarred road DOWN the hill for 0.5ml/0.8km, where a bridge crosses a small stream and the road goes up a steep incline to arrive at a crossroads. At the junction, a small national school stands in front of you with a church down to your right. NOTE: A new, but very rough, short cut is available here, being part of the Duhallow Trail. Watch for the sign on right, 500m/1,500ft after the City.

Along the way, the quiet country road wanders between the hedgerowed farms and, being blissfully free of traffic, allows one to relax and enjoy the sounds and smells of the countryside. Sweet-scented HONEYSUCKLE (*Lonicera periclymenum*) fills the lanes with its aromatic scent during the approach of autumn, BEES drone about the flowers of BLACKBERRIES in mid-summer, while ROBINS sing atop territorial posts in early spring.

(14) On arriving at the junction go to the RIGHT and pass by the church. Continue along the road for 1ml/1.6km, until the first right turn is met.

The roadside is richly adorned with trees of HAWTHORN and ASH, so watch for FIELDFARES in winter as they feed upon the HAWS, or for the scavenging MAGPIES in early spring, scouring the hedgerow for unattended nests. The magpie's domed nest of twigs can sometimes be spotted in the upper branches of ASH and other trees before the leaves develop.

(15) Take the RIGHT turn, which has concrete fencing posts at its junction with the road. You are now back on the Sloigeadal road, so follow it all the way home.

At first, the road wanders up between several houses and you get the odd glimpse of the Paps over to the right. Eventually, the houses are left behind and the road slowly climbs up and out of the more fertile lowlands to the wilder terrain of the mountains ahead.

(16) After the last of the houses, a steel gate is met. Pass through (reclose) and continue UP into the glen along the stony track.

Within the glen, rocks and boulders tumble down the slope on your left, while ahead on your right is the picturesque Glannafreaghaun Lake ('glen of the whortle berries') or Shrone Lake, hiding beneath the high cliffs of the eastern Pap. Here, RAVENS kite and glide, spiralling up on rising air currents to the ledges upon which they begin to nest as early as February.

Wild creatures are not and were not the only ones to find sanctuary in the high crevasses. During the Troubles of 1916, many a youth hid here from the bullets of the infamous Black and Tans. One old gentleman, still living next to the City, recounts how, as a boy, he fled from the soldiers to this spot. Pressing himself close to the ground, the youth and his mate lay on a high cliff ledge for the entire day while a spotter plane scouted close to the cliffs above their heads and marksmen with loaded rifles walked within feet of where they lay. Sad times that are hard to visualise now as you wander silently through the picturesque glen.

(17) Further along the glen, the expanse of boggy heath stretches down towards the lake on your right.

Normally poor in birdlife, it does attract the HERON and the CORMORANT during spring and early summer. In winter, you may spot the passage migrant and see anything from WHOOPER SWANS to GREAT NORTHERN DIVERS dropping in for a rest. Try to ignore the discarded rubbish along the track. Obviously, many see these beautiful wild places as being totally without value.

(18) The track climbs UP out of the back of the glen, through another gate, and you arrive at the wood where you made your original ascent.

(3) Keep STRAIGHT on to arrive back at your car (1).

3 – Mangerton

LOCATION: Travel south from Killarney town on the Kenmare road for 2ml/3.2km and take the signposted LEFT turn just beyond Muckross Park Hotel. Continue for another 1ml/1.6km and then take the next RIGHT turn with a sign for Mangerton 1.25ml/2.5km. Follow this road until the car park is met.

TERRAIN: A tough circular walk that makes a gradual but steep rise to the top of Mangerton Mountain (2756ft/835m). The route follows a rough path up through the mountainous heath. For the experienced only.

FEATURES: Mountain heath; lake and peaks.

LENGTH: 6ml/10km.

TIME: 5hrs.

EQUIPMENT: Strong walking boots, windproof and rainproof jacket.

WHEN TO WALK: Any time of the year when the weather is dry and there is no risk of low cloud or mist.

WALK OUTLINE

(**1**) From the car park, CONTINUE along the road to a bend where a concrete bridge crosses over the Finoulagh river.

(**2**) Cross the bridge and follow the path's outline, first by the river and then, after you go through a gate, UP through the open heath. The path disappears and reappears several times, but becomes more distinct towards the top, and eventually leads to the concrete dam at the Devil's Punch Bowl outlet.

(**3**) At the dam, leave the track and go to the LEFT of the lake, climbing up the steep boulder-strewn incline of the mountain until the cliffed ridge is reached.

(**4**) Continue along the ridge, gradually swinging around to the RIGHT and up to the summit cairn on the top.

(**5**) Leaving the summit, continue to walk around the Punch Bowl and down the other side.

(**3**) Rejoin the track beyond the dam at the lake's outlet and return by the outward route to the car park.

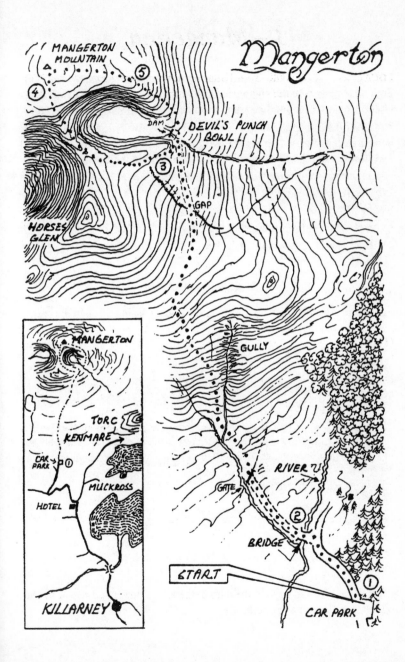

4 – Torc Mountain

LOCATION: 4ml/6.5km from Killarney town on the Kenmare road. Take the first LEFT beyond the motor car entrance to Muckross House and Gardens and drive up through the woods to the car park.

TERRAIN: A moderate one-way walk to the top of a high peak that gives commanding views over the Killarney lakes. The route follows a well-outlined path and is suitable for anyone who is fit and agile.

FEATURES: Coniferous woods; mountain heath; panoramic views.

LENGTH: 4ml/6.5km.

TIME: 2.5–3hrs.

EQUIPMENT: Comfortable walking boots with a good grip.

WHEN TO WALK: Any time of the year, but not to be attempted in low cloud or mist.

WALK OUTLINE

(1) From the car park, walk UP along the track, passing through the barrier, and continue on STRAIGHT until the river is met.

(2) Cross the Owengarriff river at the bridge and go to the LEFT, passing through a gate.

(3) On climbing the hill you pass through a gap. Keep on STRAIGHT for another 820ft/250m out onto the more open heath. Keep an eye out for a rough cutting into the heath on your right.

(4) On reaching a hill top after 820ft/250m, watch for a rough footpath that branches off to the RIGHT. This will have a heap of stones near it and beside a cutting in the turf bank. Follow the path as it zigzags its way to the top of Torc Mountain (1,764ft/525m).

(5) The path goes towards the west initially and nearer the top swings to the RIGHT. On reaching the top return by the outward route.

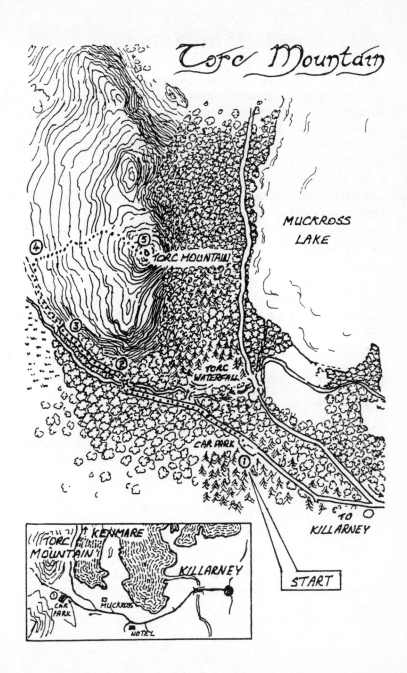

5 – Knockreer

LOCATION: The walk starts and ends in Killarney town, beginning in the Knockreer demesne opposite the town's imposing cathedral.

TERRAIN: A casual circular walk, suitable for all, but with one very muddy laneway.

FEATURES: Wooded demesne; Ross Castle; Killarney lakes.

LENGTH: 5ml/8km.

TIME: 3hrs.

EQUIPMENT: Comfortable walking boots.

WHEN TO WALK: Any time of the year.

WALK OUTLINE

(1) Cross over the stone bridge into the estate and pass the thatched Deenagh Lodge which you keep on your right. Take the first path down to your LEFT, cross over the King's Bridge and turn RIGHT immediately.

(2) Continue along the riverside path until you reach the White Bridge. Here, turn LEFT, following the signposted route to Ross Castle.

(3) At a Y-junction go to the RIGHT, following the sign for Ross Castle.

(4) At the next signposted junction, turn LEFT for Ross Castle.

(5) From Ross Castle return to point (4) and go to the LEFT.

(6) When the track reaches a river, go to the LEFT, over the bridge.

(7) At a muddy stile, pass through and follow the grassy footpath up to a tarred road, maintaining a STRAIGHT line to arrive at a T-junction.

(8) At the T-junction, go to the RIGHT.

(9) On reaching a gate pass through and continue on STRAIGHT to a Y-junction where you go down to the RIGHT. Gradually work your way around to the LEFT to reach the gardens of Knockreer House, ignoring the private entrances on the right.

(10) Walk through the gardens and around to the front of the house, following the avenue out and down to the RIGHT to reach the start of the walk.

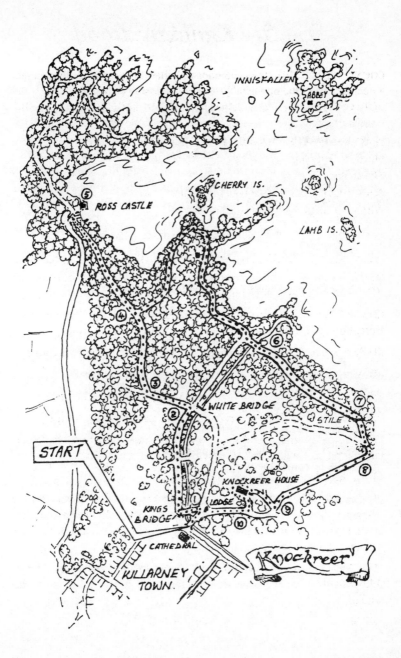

INNISFALLEN

ABBEY

CHERRY IS.

⑤ ROSS CASTLE

LAMB IS.

④

⑥

③

⑦

② WHITE BRIDGE

STILE

START

⑧

KNOCKREER HOUSE

① LODGE ⑨

KINGS BRIDGE ⑩

CATHEDRAL

Knockreer

KILLARNEY TOWN.

6 – Old Kenmare Road

LOCATION: 4mls/6.5 km from the town of Killarney on the Kenmare road. Take the first left beyond the main entrance to Muckross House and Gardens and follow this side road up to the carpark.

TERRAIN: A moderate one-way walk along an old track that leads all the way to Kenmare town. In parts this becomes boggy and waterlogged but is quite accessible for everybody. Arrange for a pick-up at Kenmare.

LENGTH: The total length of the old road is 10mls/16km. OPTION: A shorter walk, 8ml/13km, in which you return to the starting point, can be had by walking as far as the footbridge over the Galways river at point (4) and returning by the same route.

TIME: One-way walk to Kenmare, 5hrs. OPTION: 4hrs.

EQUIPMENT: Comfortable walking boots; wellingtons desirable in wet weather.

WHEN TO WALK: Suitable at any time of the year.

WALK OUTLINE

(1) From the car park follow the old road UPWARDS, cross the timber bridge, swing LEFT and later pass through a gate on to the open moors.

(2) The track is clearly outlined for most of its length and a simple footbridge carries you across the river below Cores cascades.

(3) On reaching Esknamucky Glen, the path continues UP through the woods and out again on to more heath.

(4) Soon the woods return and the path leads you down to the Galways river, with its sturdy footbridge.

You have now travelled approximately 4mls/6.5km, and you may wish to simply turn around and return by the same route. However, if you are going all the way to Kenmare, cross the footbridge and follow the path STRAIGHT ahead through the woods.

(5) The path emerges onto boggy heath and then out onto a tarred road, where you go LEFT. Follow this route through the wild uplands all the way to Kenmare.

(6) When the track arrives at a tarred road at a junction, keep going STRAIGHT, and you will go direct to Kenmare (7).

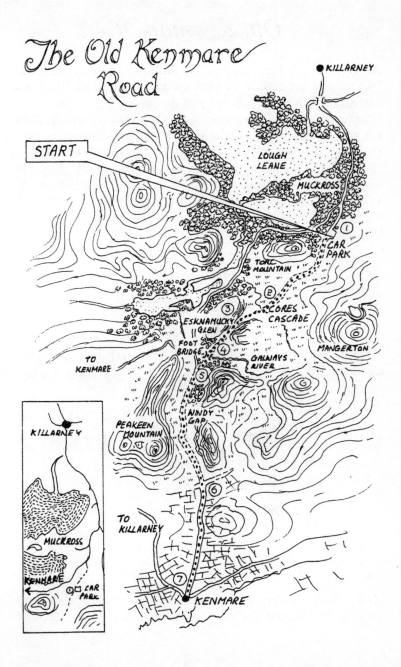

The Old Kenmare Road

7 – Crohane

LOCATION: Travelling from Killarney, take the Kenmare road for 2ml/3.2km and take the LEFT turn off for Lough Guitane, just before Muckross village. Watch for a lane on the RIGHT 0.25ml/0.4km beyond Lough Guitane and surrounded by conifer trees, just after the brow of a hill. Park the car here on the roadside.

TERRAIN: A tough one-way walk to the peak of Crohane Mountain. At first a well-defined track, it later opens out onto the mountain heath which rises gradually to the summit (2162ft/656m).

FEATURES: Mountain heath; panoramic views.

LENGTH: 4ml/6.5km.

TIME: 4hrs.

EQUIPMENT: Strong mountain boots and weatherproof clothing during cold and windy weather.

WHEN TO WALK: Needs a clear, dry day, when there is no risk of low cloud or mist descending on the mountain top.

WALK OUTLINE

(1) Follow the laneway upwards, passing a number of houses on the way.

(2) On reaching a gate and sheep-pen, pass through and continue to follow the track to its very end.

(3) Climb upwards to the summit of Crohane, veering gradually to the left.

(4) On reaching the summit return by the outward route to the parked car.

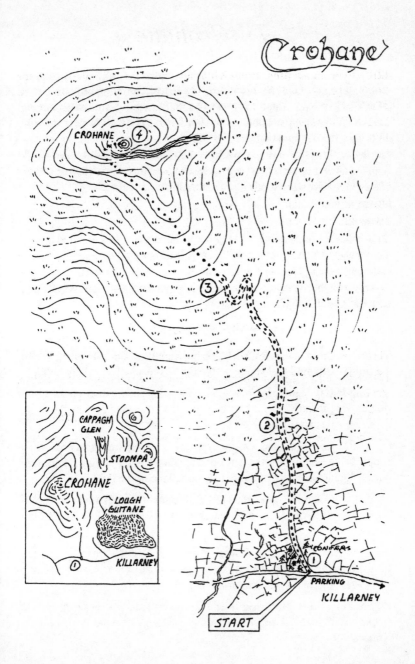

Crohane

CAPPAGH GLEN
STOOMPA
CROHANE
LOUGH GUITANE
KILLARNEY

CROHANE

CONIFERS
PARKING
KILLARNEY

START

8 – Tomies Wood

LOCATION: On the Killarney to Killorglin road, take the signposted LEFT turn for the Gap of Dunloe. Continue for 1.5ml/2.5km to a T-junction, then go LEFT. Follow this road to its very end at the shoreline of Lough Leane. Here, there is a group of houses and it is the only practical place to park, but please do so with consideration for others.

TERRAIN: A casual circular walk through oak woods, suitable for all. However, there is one stream to be crossed via some crude stepping stones.

FEATURES: Fine oak woods; views over Killarney lakes.

LENGTH: 6ml/9.5km.

TIME: 3hrs.

EQUIPMENT: Comfortable walking boots, but wellingtons required during wet weather when a mountain stream will be difficult to cross.

WHEN TO WALK: Not very suitable during the peak summer season as the parking area becomes crowded. After heavy rain the stream in the wood may not be fordable.

WALK OUTLINE

(1) From your parked car, walk back along the road for about 0.25ml/0.4km, until an avenue on the LEFT is reached at a sharp bend.

(2) Turn into the LEFT and follow the pedestrian access through the farm, first passing through a stile by a gate and later a second gate by the farm. Close all gates after you.

(3) A third gate is reached with an iron stile. Pass through, crossing over a simple bridge and follow the lane up to the RIGHT of the National Park sign until a Y-junction is met. Ignore the rough lane to the left.

(4) At the Y-junction, go to the LEFT and follow the track into the woods. To view O'Sullivan's Cascade, watch for a lane on the LEFT, 1ml/1.6km ahead.

(5) On reaching the lane, follow it down for 164ft/50m, then take a footpath on the RIGHT down into the gorge. Be careful of the steep incline. After viewing the cascade, return to (5).

(6) Presently the track crosses over a timber bridge and CONTINUES to rise steeply with panoramic views out over Lough Leane and towards Killarney town.

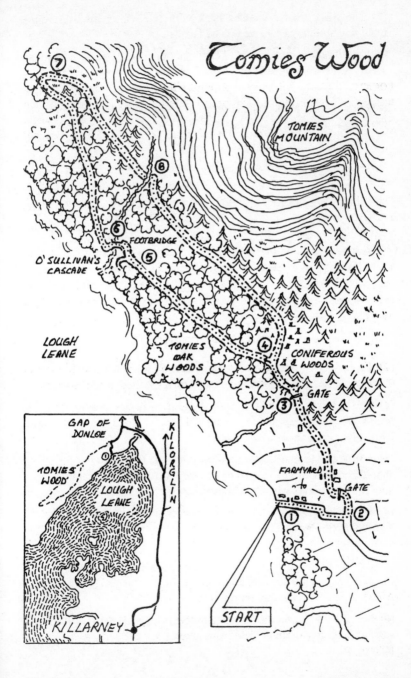

(7) The track finally doubles back with fine views towards Tomies mountain and the expansive upland heath.

(8) Cross the stream by means of the large stepping stones or simply wade across if the water is low. (If it is in flood do not cross but return by the outward route.)

(4) On returning to the Y-junction go to the LEFT and follow the outward route back to the car (1).

9 – Lough Acoose

THE MOUNTAINOUS REGIONS OF KERRY, older than the Himalayas and the Alps, have the history of their four hundred million years etched into their contorted folds. Parts of the Blasket Islands, for example, are the result of laval flows, Mangerton Mountain in Killarney is what remains of an extinct volcano, Carrauntoohil, Ireland's highest mountain, is an upheaval fold from an earthquake and the Gap of Dunloe is a glaciated valley; moreover, Killarney town sits on an old seabed and the now fertile plains around the Shannon were once covered in steaming tropical forests full of crocodiles. Though it may be difficult to distinguish some of these features, the results of ancient earthquakes and of four ice ages can be well observed about the foot of the largest mountain of them all, Carrauntoohil. Very much a worn-down stump of its former size, it is still a formidable mountain and one that is really accessible only to the more experienced climber. Temperatures at its top are ten degrees lower than in the lowlands. Parts of its steep slopes are covered in treacherous loose scree. Precipitous cliffs soar above deep corried lakes and winter flash floods in its upland rivers and streams can be devastating in their impact. Thus it is beyond the reach of the more casual walker. However, its haunting splendour can be

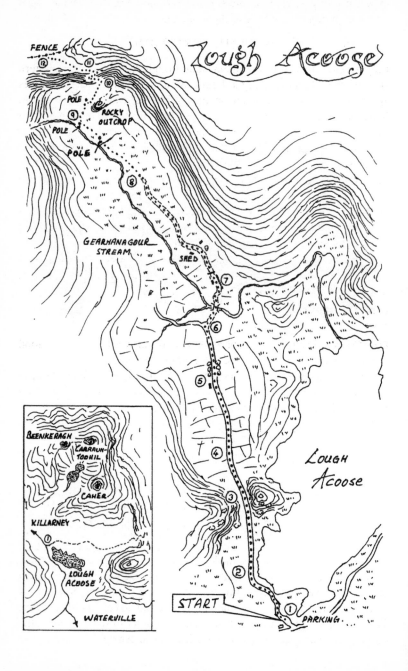

Lough Acoose

FENCE
⑫ ⑪
POLE
⑩
ROCKY OUTCROP
POLE
⑨
POLE
POLE
⑧
GEARHANAGOUR STREAM
SHED
⑦
⑥
⑤
④
③
②
START
①
PARKING

LOUGH
ACOOSE

BEENKERAGH
CARRAUN-TOOHIL
CAHER
KILLARNEY
①
LOUGH
ACOOSE
WATERVILLE

experienced by walking an old route called the Lack Road, which runs over a high ridge at the base of the mountain.

WALK DESCRIPTION

LOCATION: Adjacent to the picturesque Lough Acoose, on the western side of the Macgillycuddy's Reeks mountain range. The lough is approximately 8ml/13km from the town of Killorglin or 16ml/27km from Killarney on the scenic Glencar road to Waterville. At the lough a small road with a house nearby goes up to the LEFT. A limited amount of parking is available along the sides of this road, but please leave room for the residents living at the end of this roadway.

TERRAIN: A tough one-way walk up to a high ridge (1200ft/365m) following the outline of the old road. This road has become very dilapidated towards its end, thus it is suitable only for the more experienced walker, who is reasonably fit and appropriately equipped. Not suitable for small children or the first-time walker.

FEATURES: Spectacular mountain scenery with views of Carrauntoohil, Ireland's highest mountain; moorland heath and wildlife; Ice Age features; lakeshore wildlife.

LENGTH: 5ml/8km.

TIME: 3hrs.

EQUIPMENT: Strong waterproof walking boots or wellingtons with good grip; knapsack to carry food and a wind/rainproof jacket.

WHEN TO WALK: Pick a fine clear day with little chance of low cloud or rain. Keep wrapped up during windy weather as the area is open and exposed, especially during the winter months.

WALK OUTLINE

(1) Walk UP the narrow road that follows the edge of the lake.

Lough Acoose stretches out across the highland valley to merge with the expanses of heath which pour down the sides of the besieging rocky hills. On your left, the three high peaks of Beenkeragh (3314ft/1003m), Carrauntoohil (3414ft/1034m – the highest point in Ireland) and Caher (3200ft/970m), poke into the sky.

(2) The road weaves AROUND the lakeshore, passing the scrubby heath of FURZE and HEATHER. The diversity of heathland flora is generally reduced for several reasons: a lack of minerals in the acidic soil, the high level of leaching caused by excessive amounts of rain, and its vulnerability to fire. Thus, any plants present have had to adapt in order to survive. Here, the ordinary heather, for example, has tiny leaves which help trap the diffused

Batterswoet.

The butterwort sends up its tall stand of purple flowers in early summer, and is primarily confined to this part of Ireland.

light that occurs in these cloudy overcast islands, and its roots are able to withstand a certain amount of burning (from gorse fires), a feature which allows it to regenerate. On a more spectacular scale, there is the GIANT BUTTERWORT (*Pinguicula grandifolia*), an insect eater. Its leaves, which trap prey, glisten with ensnaring juices and are sticky to touch. Its deep violet flowers appear in June and its lime-green leaves spread out in a basal rosette that make it easily recognisable. In such mineral-impoverished soil, insects are the only available source of nitrogen-rich protein with which these plants can build their tissues.

(3) As you move UP towards a pass in the rocks, stunted HOLLY trees grow from the inaccessible cracks, well out of reach of grazing SHEEP. The woodlands of the surrounding valleys would once have reached this height. Further down, in the valley of Glencar, are the remains of one of the smelting works built by the Petty family in the eighteenth century, as outlined in the Muckross walk. Fired by the massive OAK forests that cloaked the countryside, these works were the cause of the wood's demise and turned the uplands into wild barren tracts of heath.

(4) Further on, the inner depths of the valley unfold, and some small farmed fields nestle amongst the harsher terrain, under siege from the encroaching BRACKEN FERN.

Several types of GRASSHOPPER can be heard on the finer sunny days, especially near the grassy parts of heathland. There are few varieties of animal species in these wild parts, but again certain types have adapted well in their bid to survive. One such group is the many and varied forms of invertebrates (creepy crawlies!). The heathland scrub of HEATHER, GORSE and BROOM is full of predatory SPIDERS, while many predatory DRAGONFLIES are seen on the wing. Predatory spiders do not make a web, but lie in wait within flowers for the smaller insects, pouncing on them when they show up. MOTHS and BUTTERFLIES are not well represented here, save for a few dull brown-coloured ringlets like the MEADOW BROWN and GATEKEEPER.

(5) Soon you pass a low farmhouse on the left and the road goes through a tunnel of SILVER BIRCH trees. Look closely at the tight round knots of twigs hanging from the tree branches.

The gatekeeper, though more frequent in the lowlands, will still be found in sunny laneways, especially if there are blackberries about.

Though these look like birds' nests, they are, in fact, a form of cankerous growth unique to this tree, and fortunately not fatal.

(6) When the road arrives at a Y junction, go to the RIGHT.

The road now becomes an earthen track that leads down to a bridge over the Gearhanagour stream. Like most upland streams, this is poor in nutrients because of the impervious nature of the old red sandstone rocks. Thus, the number of aquatic insects is low and so little bird life can derive a livelihood from it. Any birds that may be seen are dependent on the rich insect pickings available in the surrounding heath. Birds most likely to be encountered are the resilient winter SNIPE, with, in summer, birds of the uplands such as WHEATEARS, STONECHATS, CURLEW and SKYLARKS.

(7) The track passes between some abandoned stone buildings, then through a gate up to a working farmyard. The lane continues on the RIGHTHAND side of the galvanised shed visible ahead.

On a bend in the laneway beyond the shed, a fine view into the back of the valley appears. The whole valley was gouged out by a glacier that ground down the rocks as it poured from the mountain tops. The summits of the Macgillycuddy's Reeks would have projected above the ice sheets, their sides being shattered into dizzy slopes of scree by the glaciers, to leave behind the pointed and jagged peaks. Extensive piles of this loose rock can be seen against the steep gradient of Caher Mountain. As a result of the extreme temperatures and the loose rocks, plants generally seen in

The stonechat, with its distinctive black head, may be
seen on top of a bushy perch as it scans the
surrounding heath.

the high Alps or the Arctic, such as STARRY SAXIFRAGE (*Saxifraga stellaris*), ALPINE CLUBMOSS(*Lycopodium alpinum*) and MOUNTAIN SORREL (*Oxyria digyna*), can be found surviving on the freezing slopes of Carrauntoohil, survivors perhaps from the post Ice Age era when Ireland was a land of tundra.

(8) As you near the riverside, the track begins to peter out and conditions underfoot start to roughen. However, follow the bank UPWARDS, crossing a small stream by way of some crude stepping stones, until the second of two 'Kerry Way' marker poles is met by the river bank.

The Gearhanagour stream courses straight across the rocky valley bottom, coming down from the top of Caher Mountain through a gradient of 2500ft/760m. It is ice cold and subject to frequent flash floods in winter rains which can surge across the valley floor. As you near the loftier cliffed peaks in front of you and on your right, the call of RAVENS echoes across the coombe. Soaring over the uplands, these are primarily scavenging birds which feed on the carrion of dead SHEEP and other hapless victims of the harsh terrain. Brilliant aerobatics take place in the sky during the early spring courtship displays, after which they nest among the inaccessible ledges of the high cliffs.

(9) At the second marker pole, go to the RIGHT, keeping to the left of the large rocky outcrop and climbing up through the rough and boulder-strewn terrain until another marker pole is met. There is no real path to follow, but keep going towards the cliffs up in front and slightly to the left.

As you clamber over the rocks, you may be lucky enough to spot the well-known but little-seen KERRY SLUG (*Geomalacus maculosus*). This grey-green creamy-spotted animal prefers to wander out when the weather is wet. A rarity found only in the extreme south-west, it is another oddity and is more at home in northern Portugal. It belongs to the mysterious Lusitanian group, which it is argued dates from before the Ice Age and possibly survived in unglaciated pockets of the mountains. To make matters that bit more complicated, you may find the slug beside another bunch of misplaced plants, this time from North America. Look out for the pretty

Blue-eyed grass is one of the many rare and unusual plants found growing in the wet meadows and heaths of Kerry. Flowering in late summer, its more characteristic habitat is the temperate regions of North America.

flowered BLUE-EYED GRASS (*Sisyrinchium angustifolium*), which has its headquarters here in the south-west upland regions. All in all, enough puzzles lie scattered about these hills to keep any botanist busy.

(10) On reaching the cliff base, a Kerry Way marker pole amidst a jumble of rocky outcrops should show you the point at which you climb up along the rough outline of the old track to the LEFT. The climb will be awkward and difficult for the less experienced, and care should be taken as you zigzag up the wet and muddy rocks. However, you should meet two further poles on the way up which will help you maintain your direction.

(11) As you climb, the view behind you expands out beyond Lough Acoose and the mountainous nature of the terrain looms large across the horizon.

If here in winter, you may be surprised to see an OWL in these parts. The area is visited by migrant SHORT-EARED OWLS (*Asio flammeus*), a sub-Arctic species that moves south in search of rodents during harsh winters. Recognised by their brownish streaked appearance, they are very much a bird of prey of the open moorlands and do not frequent wooded areas.

(12) Reaching the top of the rough incline, you find the boggy heath goes at an angle to the LEFT and a fence is reached.

You have now arrived at the top of the ridge and the walk's end. However, by crossing the stile you can follow the track down into the next valley or just clamber about the rocks to take in the views. The valley on the other side is also deeply glaciated and spectacular views of the surrounding mountains rise up on all sides.

(1) Return by the same route to the start of the walk.

10 – Bray Head

KERRY, WITH ITS MANY peninsulas poking out into the Atlantic, offers numerous opportunities to watch the workings of the sea against the grandeur of its mountainous terrain. Many of these wild, forlorn peninsulas are free of modern bungalow blight and unsympathetic tourist developments. They possess a sense of unattached freedom and release in their wild abandoned bleakness that haunts and yet draws upon one's spirit. On Bray Head an ancient road winds and weaves around the rocky terrain and meanders between stone-walled fields as it leads you on and up to the final precipice. Age-old settlements skirt the roadside margins and lie scattered about the fields, evoking memories of other times, other civilisations. Choughs career and glide across upland heath, calling wildly over the thunder of pounding waves beating against the crumbling cliffs far below you, while wind-scoured hills are flushed with the radiant glow of yellow gorse and purple heather.

WALK DESCRIPTION

LOCATION: Bray Head sits at the western end of Valentia Island, on the northern tip of the Iveragh peninsula and near the picturesque town of Caherciveen.

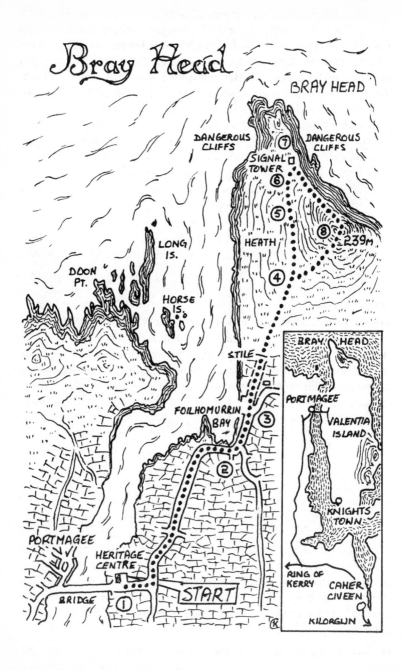

Bray Head

BRAY HEAD

DANGEROUS CLIFFS

DANGEROUS CLIFFS

⑦

SIGNAL TOWER

⑥

⑤

⑧ 239m

LONG IS.

HEATH

DOON PT.

④

HORSE IS.

STILE

FOILHOMURRIN BAY

③

②

PORTMAGEE

HERITAGE CENTRE

START

BRIDGE

①

BRAY HEAD

PORTMAGEE

VALENTIA ISLAND

KNIGHTS TOWN

RING OF KERRY

CAHER CIVEEN

KILORGLIN

The walk begins from the car park of the Heritage Centre, accessible by bridge from the small village of Portmagee. Follow the N70 from Caherciveen towards Waterville and after 3ml/5km take the R565 on the RIGHT, signposted for Portmagee and Valentia. Crossing the bridge onto the island by Portmagee, the Heritage Centre is on your immediate LEFT. There is ample car parking space here during the summer months. However, this will be closed during the winter, when you may prefer to park within the environs of Portmagee.

TERRAIN: A casual, one-way walk along the Atlantic coast of the island. This follows a section of tarred road at the start, and later a rough track, which leads out and up to the open moors of the headland.

WARNING: Please note that there are exposed and exceedingly high cliffs at the walk's end. These are dangerous for the unwary and are not suitable for children or those with a fear of heights.

FEATURES: Magnificent sea views; coastal heath and wildlife; ancient religious site; ring fort; spectacular cliffs; internationally renowned bird sanctuaries.

LENGTH: 5ml/8km.

TIME: 3hrs.

EQUIPMENT: Comfortable walking shoes and windproof jacket, as the road is rather exposed to the sea. Binoculars are an advantage.

WHEN TO WALK: Suitable at any time of the year. However, not advisable during stormy or windy weather, when the cliffs are at their most dangerous. Neither is it suitable when coastal fog or low clouds shroud the high-cliffed peak at the walk's end.

WALK OUTLINE

(1) Leaving the car park of the Heritage Centre, turn to the LEFT and follow the road up to the T-junction (with signposts), where you again turn to the LEFT. Continue along this narrow country road for the next mile or so, going to the LEFT for a third time at another Y-junction (also with signposts). Ignore the smaller side roads into private houses.

The road skirts beside the sea, looking out over the entrance to Portmagee Channel. Along the way the monotony of small farmed fields and grass-smothered hedgerows belies the beauty that lies ahead. These fields, sheltered by the northern hills, harbour many birds during the late summer. Watch for FINCHES, LARKS, PIPITS and STARLINGS rising in crowded flocks from their seed- and insect-probing forays at your approach.

(2) On reaching the Y-junction, which teeters above the wave-lashed cove

The 6in/15cm long 'mermaid's purse' is actually the egg case of the common skate *(Raja batis)*, a coastal-dwelling ray that can be up to 6ft/2m in length.

of Foilhomurrin Bay, go to the LEFT. Continue for several hundred metres (0.25ml) and keep an eye out for a lane branching off to the LEFT, which passes up through a lay-by that hangs above the sea.

Though not accessible during wild weather, the small cove of Foilhomurrin Bay does throw out its own delights. After a storm various bits of debris get cast up on the surrounding fields. You may come across anything from a beached JELLYFISH to the discarded egg cases of SHARKS and RAYS. The latter are more commonly known as 'mermaids' purses', their shape suggesting some such item. A couple of inches in length, these flat, rectangular, leathery pouches have long tendrils hanging from their four corners. Though you may never get to see a ray or a shark, these common enough egg cases testify to their presence in our offshore waters.

(3) Presently the road reaches a sharp bend, with a two-storey house on its western side. Here the lane leaves the tarred road, passing up through the lay-by on the LEFT and out on to the exposed heath. A short distance up, a gate crosses the lane, but use the stile on its right to gain access to the wild moors ahead.

(4) Rising steadily upwards, the heath is stunted and shorn by the ever-present salty sea winds. This greatly restricts the variety of plants found in this exposed environment, but during the summer months several small flowers can be found about the heath. Watch for the yellow flowers of COMMON TORMENTIL *(Potentilla erecta)* and the small, blue-flowered HEATH MILKWORT *(Polygala serpyllifolia)*. More unusual plants can also be encountered, such as the BURNET ROSE *(Rosa pimpinellifolia)*, a small bushy shrub with a stem covered with a prickly layer of red, thorny hairs that bears soft, white blooms. It is a cousin to the more common DOG ROSE, found throughout the countryside, but is confined to coastal heaths and dunes. It is a diminishing species, which needs protection and should not be picked.

During the summer months, if the weather is calm, numerous moths and butterflies of the heath are regularly encountered. Of course there are a variety of other smaller insects, and none more annoying than the biting MIDGES.

(5) As the lane climbs higher and further out to the headland, better and better views of the cliffed and indented coastline to the south open up. Across the channel the shattered, rocky outlines of Horse Island and Long Island protrude from the cliffs of the mainland about Doon Point. Further south, the large, pinnacled Puffin Island, a protected bird sanctuary for numerous sea birds, floats just offshore. The shallow continental shelf that extends outwards for several hundred miles is rich in fish life and harbours an incalculable wealth of marine life. As yet unpolluted, the vast store of food draws millions of birds to the west coast of Ireland each summer. Here they breed in impressive colonies about the coastal cliffs and inaccessible island pinnacles.

Sadly, since 1949, large quantities of spent nuclear fuel (130,000 tons) have been dumped about 380ml/600km southwest of here by the nuclear industry. Its potential to enter the food chains is immense, as the containers in which it was encased will be outlived by the waste itself. The arguments of the time – that the waste would be greatly diluted by the ocean – are now shown to be false. Toxins, no matter how diluted, become very concentrated as they pass through the various food chains of nature, where, in time, they inflict horrendous damage.

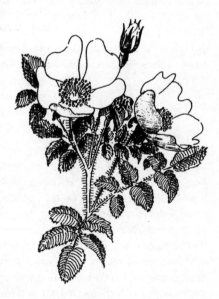

(6) Approaching the end of the lane, the ruined Napoleonic Tower comes into view. In front of the tower the lane ends and a crude path rises upwards to the RIGHT. Follow this along the cliff line up to the highest point, but keep well back from the edge.

Perched precariously atop the precipitous cliffs, it has

The burnet rose. Now diminishing in numbers, this delicate rose of coastal heaths is under threat through loss of habitat.

spectacular views out over the vastness of the Atlantic. It was used as a lookout point during the Napoleonic Wars, when England feared an invasion into Ireland from France. If a sea invasion were to occur, a message could quickly be relayed through a chain of such towers that stretched along the southern coastline, eventually reaching army headquarters in Cork.

Here cliffs surround you on all sides, and it cannot be emphasised strongly enough how DANGEROUS these are. Keep your distance from them. They are constantly battered by the ocean swell and can be prone to sudden collapse. Additionally, during windy weather, updrafts and sudden gusts of wind can catch you unawares. They should therefore be treated with the greatest of caution.

(7) An ideal place for a break and to observe the sea, keep your eyes peeled for WHALES and DOLPHINS that pass up during the spring and down during the autumn. It is also an ideal perch to observe the numerous sea birds that breed about the coastal islands during the summer.

Looking out to the southwest, the romantic rocky pinnacles of Little Skellig on the left, and the Great Skellig on the right, pierce the horizon. Little Skellig is an important breeding site for GANNETS. It ranks second in the world for sheer quantity of birds, sometimes housing in excess of 60,000 individuals. Every available ledge is occupied by birds, coating the rocks like white snowflakes. Great Skellig supports numerous breeding birds, from PUFFINS to AUKS and PETRELS. However, it is more famous for

its monastic ruins. These date back over a thousand years, to when the island was used as a spiritual retreat by Christian monks.

Unfortunately, a negative aspect of our new-found interest in nature is the fact that some visitors to the Great Skellig are also drawn to the spectacle of the nesting Gannets on Little Skellig. During the summer, boats

Rounding a bend in the road, the ruined signal tower beckons one onwards to the high cliffs of Bray Head.

filled with sightseers sail too near to the cliffs, causing the nesting birds to panic, and in their sudden charge from the nest, unhatched eggs fall from the cliff ledges. Consequently numbers are beginning to fall, demonstrating how sensitive our interest in the outdoors must be.

Formed of ancient Old Red Sandstone, and once part of an extensive Iveragh peninsula, the now isolated and inhospitable Skelligs were chosen as a spiritual retreat by Christian monks over a thousand years ago.

(8) The path rise sharply up towards the highest point at 239 metres, with the cliffs of Foilnanean (this possibly translates as the 'cliff of the birds') plummeting down to the crashing waves far below. Having reached the summit, turn to the RIGHT and slowly descend the steep hill to pick up the lane again at point (4).

Fabulous views stretch northwards across Dingle Bay to the long spine of the Dingle Peninsula. At its furthest extremity another cluster of famous bird colonies can be seen – the Blasket Islands. On the left is the smaller Inishvickillane, dwarfed by the larger Great Blasket on the right.

Looking up, you may see a gliding KESTREL stop in mid-air and hover over a particular spot as it watches smaller birds and mammals. It pounces suddenly, dropping from the air like a stone and just as quickly rising. The kestrel is the most common bird of prey in our countryside and has adapted well to the presence of humans. It will often be seen sitting on telegraph wires near human habitations and, in some cases, has even moved into large towns and cities. But watching it comb across the heather in search of food is an incomparable experience. Only then can its acrobatic skills be fully observed and appreciated.

(4) On reaching the lane, turn to the LEFT and follow the outward route back to the car.

As you head back, you will notice that the small meadows on either side of you are free from the effects of intensive agriculture and so can support a wide variety of wild flowers. In spring, carpets of DAISIES cover the fields; these in time are replaced by the yellow of BUTTERCUPS and the red of CLOVER. Several insects will be flushed out as you pass. However, it is only when the HEATHER and GORSE come into bloom in late summer that the real riches of these wild gardens become evident. Then, insects rise at every step and the fattening SKYLARKS take to the wing. If it is a good summer and insects are really plentiful, the skylark may produce as many as three separate broods.

11 – Lough Currane

AT THE END OF THE IVERAGH PENINSULA a thin strip of land and fresh water lies sandwiched between the steep mountainous heaths and the nearby ocean surf. From the broad stretch of the mountains, a clutter of small streams and rivers flows downwards to become ensnared in a deep and expansive lake before emptying into the sea. These waters attract and support large numbers of sea trout and salmon because of the rich populations of insects found in the unpolluted waterways, so the area is very much the haunt of the fisherman and fisherwoman. Set in a stunning arena of high mountains, the beautiful lake of Lough Currane has become known to anglers throughout the world.

Around its shores, stony heaths run down from the hills to meet the reed-fringed water's edge where brown trout hide and, in summer, the mayfly rise in great swarms. But this rich wildlife is not confined to the lake – a similarly prolific and healthy assemblage of animal and plant life is to be found in the surrounding wild and mountainous environs. Throughout the winter, the coastal and sheltered waters of nearby Ballinskelligs Bay are full of migrant sea birds, while the mountain folds hide many tarns and corrie lakes in and above the glaciated valleys.

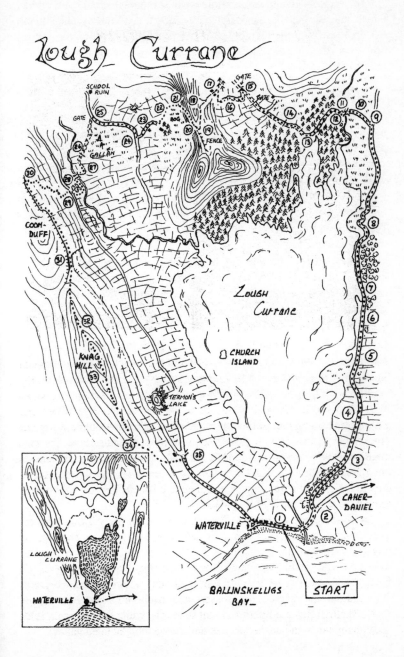

Lough Currane

SCHOOL RUIN
GATE
GATE
BOG
GALLÁN
FENCE
COOM-DUFF
Lough Currane
CHURCH ISLAND
KNAG HILL
TERMON'S LAKE
CAHER-DANIEL
WATERVILLE
BALLINSKELLIGS BAY
START

LOUGH CURRANE
WATERVILLE

Here, on isolated and inaccessible islands, remnants of old oak woods, which have escaped the hands of the tree cutter, can still be found. Around the great cliffs, birds of prey glide above a kaleidoscope of colourful blossoms stretched across the many bogs. Truly a magical place which, once visited, will call you back to explore another day.

WALK DESCRIPTION

LOCATION: The walk begins and ends in the village of Waterville, which looks out onto the picturesque Ballinskelligs Bay at the end of the Iveragh peninsula.

TERRAIN: A fairly long, tough, circular walk, but one that follows a well-defined path throughout most of its length. At first, the route follows a tarred road, then an old cattle track, which crosses rocky moors and, at times, the wet heath, to lead back into Waterville by means of the Kerry Way walking route. It is suitable for those who are reasonably fit and are used to a longer trek.

FEATURES: Lough Currane; splendid mountain scenery; wild heathland and associated wildlife; old cattle track; abandoned settlements; pre-Christian stone fort; riverside trek; section of the Kerry Way.

LENGTH: 14ml/22.5km.

TIME: 8hrs.

EQUIPMENT: Comfortable walking boots for the tarred roads, but Wellingtons essential for the wet heath during winter or after periods of much rain; knapsack to carry a supply of food and liquid. During rainy weather waterproof leggings are desirable.

WHEN TO WALK: Suitable at any time of the year. During the summer months, the initial part of the route carries a certain amount of motorised tourist traffic, thus care should be exercised when walking along the tarred road. However, as you should start out early in the morning you may be unaffected by this.

WALK OUTLINE

(1) Having parked in the village of Waterville, walk along the tarred road that leads south to Caherdaniel. Proceed until you arrive at the first turn to the LEFT, after 0.25ml/0.4km.

Beyond the village, you cross over a fine old stone bridge that arches over the river exiting from Lough Currane. Upstream, numerous fishing boats dock between the deep beds of COMMON REED (*Phragmities australis*), which produce decorative seed heads during the autumn months.

The hart's tongue fern is easily distinguished from all the other ferns by its undivided single-bladed fronds.

(2) On arriving at the LEFT turn, take the tarred road down between the few houses and later past the hotel. CONTINUE to follow it for the next few miles to point (9), while the road meanders along the impressive shoreline of the lake.

By the hotel entrance, twisted SYCAMORE and CHESTNUT trees overhang the road, their shade encouraging the growth of many ferns like the waxy single-leafed, HART'S TONGUE (*Asplenium scolopendrium*), and the tooth-leafed POLYPODY (*Polypodium vulgare*), both of which grow from the crumbling old stone walls.

(3) Emerging from the trees, you see the lake on your left, with its fine backdrop of mountain peaks visible across the wide stretch of water.

The lake was originally called Lough Lee and is said to have been formed by a great cloud burst, which was part of a tremendous storm conjured up by the ancient druids of the mythical Celtic race, Tuatha Dé Danann, in an attempt to destroy the invading sons of Milesius in 1300 BC. Many were subsequently drowned, with one son, Ir, perishing on the rocks of the Skelligs and another, Donn, on the Bull rock.

(4) Along the way, small meadows run up to meet the approaching heath on the right, their hedgerows decked with FUCHSIA bushes that sport their red lantern flowers from the months of June to September. This shrub is not native and was originally introduced as a hedging plant. It has since become naturalised throughout the southwest and, in some places, is virtually synonymous with Kerry.

(5) Eventually the road passes close to the lakeshore, where a large cliffed rock overhangs the road and out of which a twisted and stunted OAK grows.

Straight across the water, the distant outline of the small Church Island can be discerned. Opposite this island, close to your shoreline, but submerged beneath the waters of the lake, a castle is reputed to stand. According to local history, it became a victim of the steep rise in the level of the lake over the intervening centuries.

(6) Ahead, the hills begin to loom larger, with their lower slopes bearing small wooded copses of SILVER BIRCH.

By the roadside, wild ANGELICA (*Angelica sylvestris*) and MEADOW SWEET (*Filipendula ulmaria*), choke the damper drains and ditches. Both are tall plants, but the latter is more recognisable with its creamy-white fluffy flower heads having a familiar sweet smell.

(7) On approaching a woody stretch of the road overhung with OAK and HAZEL, you find many fishing boats moored among the reeds at the water's edge.

Here, a delightful vista stretches across the lake towards the distant mountain. In the early hours of the morning, it is a favourite haunt of the long-legged grey HERON (*Ardea cinerea*). A predator of small fish such as MINNOW and other fry, herons are disliked by some people, who fear that they may deplete fish stocks if their numbers become too large. However, as any good fisherperson will tell you, the presence of these birds is very important to the life of rivers and lakes, indicating that the ecosystem is in a healthy state. Other indicators are the presence of DIVING SHAGS, CORMORANTS and OTTERS. Once these species at the top of the food chains begin to disappear, it is a clear signal that some form of pollution is destroying the complex life support systems of the freshwater habitat.

(8) The road continues to wind its way through the rocky terrain, and eventually leads up onto a rise to give fine views over the entire lake, showing its upper end to be studded with numerous rocky islands.

The long glaciated valley, from which the lake emerges, stretches into the distance, ending beneath the peak of Coomcallee. On your right towering cliffs rise steeply up towards Mullaghbeg, where the small white blobs of SHEEP give some impression of their true height. Down their sides, sheets of purple HEATHER and BRACKEN swirl around the boulder-strewn landscape and cascade onto the roadside verge.

(9) Eventually, a lane branches off the tarred road to the LEFT. Turn in here and follow the lane across the wilder heath. Watch for the split rock here

The low creeping English stonecrop with its succulent leaves is
easily located on rocky outcrops and dry banks.

with the HOLLY tree growing out of it, on the right-hand side of the lane.

This old route was originally a cattle track for moving herds from one
valley to the next and leads one into a wild and beautiful tract of
countryside. The area was much more heavily populated in former times,
but now holds only two occupied dwellings. The townland is known as
Cloghvoola, translated as 'the stony milking place', a name that seems
very apt on the journey ahead.

(10) Following the stony track through the heath of SEDGE and PURPLE
MOOR GRASS (*Molinia*), you cross a concrete bridge and enter a coniferous
plantation.

Along the way, exposed rocks support clumps of the fleshy-leafed
ENGLISH STONECROP (*Sedum anglicum*), which thrives on the bare
substratum of old red sandstone. Its red-white flowers emerge from June
onwards and survive the desiccating effect of the summer sun very well, as
its swollen leaves store a plentiful supply of water.

(11) As you cross the concrete bridge at the Capall river, the diving DIPPER
bird (*Cinclus cinclus*) may be spotted, as it hunts underwater for the larval
forms of MAYFLY, CADDISFLY and STONEFLY. Once it has caught some
food, it jumps out onto a stone, devours its prey and dives back in again.
Other birds that survive on the bountiful aquatic insect population are the
GREY WAGTAILS (*Motacilla cinerea*), which though grey on their backs
appear predominantly yellow. These can be seen walking atop the floating
plant vegetation, their tails perpetually bobbing up and down.

(12) On the approach to the coniferous woods, a fine line of SILVER BIRCH
trees can be seen running along the edge. Even though the flimsy leaves of
this tree pass through some colourful variations from spring to summer,

they are at their best in winter. Then, their rich red-brown crown of twigs, atop their bleached-white silvery trunks, adds an impressive display of colour to the monotonous green of the SITKA SPRUCE plantation. Passing through the coniferous plantation, watch for TITS, SISKINS and CROSSBILLS amongst the dense vegetation of the upper branches. Crossbills are easily recognisable by their enormous scissors-like beaks, which they use to crack open pine cones and winkle out the enclosed seeds.

(13) Deeper inside the wood, the track passes near a small docking point by the lakeshore.

This upper side of the lake is the haunt of the fly fisherperson, whose popular flies read like a wildlife list – mallard, bog fly, straw grouse, golden olive and the Waterville blue are among the favourites. Many people who are against blood sports dislike the practice of fishing. However, as an environmental biologist, I have the greatest respect for fishing folk. Without their ability to spot river pollution and without the strong economic argument their sport provides, most of the rivers of Ireland would be grossly polluted by now. Fishing provides a perfect example of how wise protection of our environment allows it to be used as a valuable economic resource. Perhaps some day the presence of walkers in the wilderness will also be seen as a strong economic argument for the protection of our bogs, wild heaths, old woods, dunes and sylvan countryside in all its varied forms.

The pipewort is an inconspicuous-looking water plant, with simple button-like flowers projecting from the shallow waters of lake margins in August.

(14) Later, the track climbs past some OAK and HOLLY woods and you must pass by a gate, using the stile to its left. Further on, a lane branches off to the right, ignore this and continue STRAIGHT on through another gate with a stile.

As you walk, the trees eventually give way to boggy heath and a stream runs beside the lane. Ahead, the stony slopes of the mountain are coated in parts with thick sheets of BRACKEN. This is the land of Cloghvoola. The mountainside is practically covered in a sea of white stones and it must have been a poor grazing area for cattle in earlier times.

(15) When a group of gates is reached, the lane boomerangs up behind you on the LEFT. Use the stile on the RIGHTHAND side of the gate and follow the lane up the hill between the small fields.

Behind you, catch the good view back over the more wooded landscape. Ahead, the stony heath draws ever closer and the croaking of the scavenging CARRION or GREY CROWS (*Corvus corone*), can be heard echoing above.

St. Patrick's Cabbage

Frequently seen on old walls are the red spikes, white flowers and leathery green rosettes of St Patrick's Cabbage, another plant unique to the southwest and belonging to the rare group of Lusitanian species.

(16) The lane comes to a Y-junction at the top of the hill, where there is a stone ruin. Go to the RIGHT up beside the ruin, and follow the now grass-covered track across the rushy field. The outline of the lane is still clear, however, and it is easy to trace it as it zigzags upwards towards the conifer trees.

As you climb, glimpses of the lough are visible down on your left, with the long ridge of Mullaghbeg and Cahernageeha mountains stretching out behind it. Fairly barren in appearance, these wild heaths do have a fair share of wildlife. If here in the earlier part of the year, you may be lucky to surprise the mad March HARES. During early spring, HARES (*Lepus timidus*) gather in groups and they take part in fighting displays, rising up on their hind legs and throwing punches at each other.

(**17**) On arriving at the second grove of conifers you come across a cluster of stone ruins. The way forward passes between them and continues at an angle up to the RIGHT.

As you climb, the pourings of many invisible streams resound through the heavy scattering of stones and boulders, while up above CARRION CROWS eye your approach like vultures from the watch towers of the conifers. These birds are generally disliked in the countryside, as they are believed to cause a certain amount of damage to newborn lambs, their strong beaks being adept at picking out the defenseless lambs' eyes. However, their natural role is as scavenger and they play an important part in recycling dead matter back into the food chain.

(**18**) Beyond the old abandoned farmstead, a rough Y-junction is met. Go to the LEFT here, following the poorer of the two tracks.

The way forward is now little more than a rough and soggy footpath between the heath of short DWARF FURZE (*Ulex gallii*). As you approach the top of the ridge (500ft/150m), there are good views over the other side and out towards Bolus Head on the right of the bay. Looking down towards Waterville, you can see the narrow spit that separates the fresh waters of Lough Currane from the sea water outside.

(**19**) Continue STRAIGHT along the more level ground on top of the ridge, until you reach the sheepwire fence. Do not cross the fence, but follow it down to your RIGHT, keeping it on your LEFT, as it slowly descends at the other side of the ridge.

(**20**) Further down along the fence, a rough gate with a stile is met. Climb over this and continue in a STRAIGHT line. The way down through the rocks is not very obvious and the original path is hard to find at times. It is a tricky descent thus take care and time. However, from up here you should be able to get a good idea of the general direction to be followed. Continue down along the ridge by following the same STRAIGHT diagonal line. At the bottom, skirt the boggy heath on the left by staying close to the ridge and make a circular arc towards the farmhouse in the conifer trees, which can be seen across the valley. DO NOT go straight down through the cliffed ledges (see map).

(**21**) At the bottom of the ridge, little more than a worn footpath is visible. Periodically, this becomes lost in new growth and soggy patches. However, keep going STRAIGHT until you are in line with the grove of conifers. At this point, the path begins to veer to the LEFT.

(**22**) Nearing the farmhouse, cross a small stream and then pass through dense BRACKEN ferns. After this, the path swings LEFT, then RIGHT again to pass through a stone wall and onto a more obvious track.

Up above you on the right, lost in a maze of white-lichened stone walls and a dense sea of BRACKEN, sits a fine stone fort. This is probably a defensive settlement constructed during the Bronze Age, about four thousand years ago. The fort, with its battery of stone-walls, makes an impressive and pleasing composition, commanding views down the sloping meadows towards the distant Ballinskelligs Bay.

(**23**) The track leads down to the avenue that exits from the farmhouse on your left. Go to the RIGHT, passing out through another farmyard with some delightful stone outhouses and continue up to the road.

(**24**) On reaching the top of the avenue pass out by the entrance gate and go to the RIGHT.

The road leads up, then around a LEFT-HAND bend. Further on, it passes through stretches of bog, unfortunately, some of this is now being planted with conifers. However, the heath on the left is still untouched and allows open views across the river valley towards the long ridge of Coomduff Hill. It is along the top of this ridge that the homeward journey lies, leading you back into Waterville.

(**25**) As you pass by the boggy heath, you may spot a standing stone or *gallán* (menhir) on your left. Shortly after this and around the bend, an iron gate leads onto a laneway on the LEFT. Leave the road here and pass carefully onto the lane, following its muddy tracks across the heath. WARNING: If you reach the renovated national school, you have missed the turn!

The standing stone is a legacy from our Gaelic past and not so easy to date. These stones were erected for a multitude of reasons, from burial sites to boundary markers, right through history and, unless they carry inscriptions or carvings, it is hard to ascribe any particular date to them. Walking along the laneway, you encounter fine views across the valley on the right, with the Cummeragh river coursing under an attractive stone bridge.

(**26**) Follow the lane through the gap into the next field. If the gap is blocked, climb over the wall on its left. The lane now swings up to the LEFT.

(**27**) The lane, somewhat drier, descends on the other side of the hill towards some stone ruins on the left. Here, you swing around a circular enclosure full of HOLLY trees on the RIGHT. Then make your way down into the green fields and ultimately to the river bank, after about three fields, where you will find a rustic timber foot bridge.

(28) After crossing the footbridge, go to the LEFT along the riverbank towards a sloping grove of trees. Pass through to the other side of this grove, using the decaying foot poles, and go RIGHT, up along the poorly outlined path smothered in FURZE and out across the rough meadow to the tarred road.

The river is one of the feeder streams which empty into Lough Currane, and has a full quota of fish. As a result, it draws many predators, so keep your eyes peeled for the elusive OTTER *(Lutra lutra)*. This fascinating creature is extremely wary of humans and disappears at the first sight or sound of approach. Thus, the most you are likely to see is their telltale droppings or spraints, which are black, oily and peppered with fish scales.

The otter is one of our finest and most noble mammals, but due to years of senseless persecution it makes great efforts to avoid humans and prefers to hunt at night.

(29) On arriving onto the tarred road look for the Kerry Way sign on the opposite side and well to the RIGHT of the bungalow. Follow the path up through the field and, on arriving at a laneway, cross it and follow the lane that continues STRAIGHT. At the end of the lane, go to the RIGHT.

The path now winds its way gradually up the hill, going at an angle up through heathery slopes and leading you to the top of the ridge by means of several stiles. Behind you, there are panoramic views of the distant mountains that form the southernmost end of the Magillycuddy's Reeks. Once you gain sufficient height, you may be able to see some of the deep corried loughs set in their amphitheatres of high cliffs. One of these goes by the particularly interesting name of Lough Coomcathcum, which in old Gaelic means 'the hollow of the wild cats and wolves', hinting at the type of wildlife that existed in these parts heretofore and illustrating the close association our ancestors had with nature, after whom they named many of the physical features around them.

(30) After a tough slog, you reach the ridge top, where a stile leads over a wire fence. Go to the LEFT here and follow the wire fence to the top of Coomduff (811ft/250m), keeping the fence on your right.

Since the way ahead has stunning vistas, read the basic guidelines below, put the book in your pocket and enjoy the views until (31) is reached, about 1ml/1.6km ahead. Further on are a number of stiles that lead over wire fences – some are in a shaky condition so do exercise care when climbing over them. Keep the main fence on your right as you walk along the ridge of the hill and down the other side, until you reach a lane flanked by two earthen walls.

With such open heath, there is always a good chance of seeing the hovering KESTREL as it hunts for PIPITS and SKYLARKS over the hills, so keep a sharp look-out.

(31) As you come down the other side of Coomduff Hill, the last of the stiles leads you up through a short but muddy laneway. At its other end, continue to follow the Kerry Way marker poles up to the top of Knag Hill by rising uphill to the RIGHT.

(32) Along the way, a better track joins in from the left and a number of other gates will be met. Fasten all of these properly after you and keep a STRAIGHT course. DO NOT CLIMB OVER THE GATES.

Crossing the ridge of Knag Hill, good views are visible out across the lake to Church Island. Here there is a very significant collection of early Christian artifacts, including the remains of a twelfth-century Hiberno-Romanesque church and numerous inscribed stone slabs. It has been said that a submerged zigzag causeway once connected it to the mainland, but this has since been lost to the significant rise in water levels of the lough over the centuries.

(33) As you proceed, the occasional marker pole keeps you on track. Go to the LEFT, where the lane becomes tarred.

Old stone walls are full of holes, and you may be lucky enough to encounter the STOAT. This animal is similar to the English WEASEL, which does not occur here. (Ireland's wild mammal population is quite small when compared to our neighbours' across the water; twenty-eight species exist in Ireland compared to fifty-five in Britain.) The STOAT can be recognised by its buff-brown coat and its black-tipped tail. It is an agile killer, capable of catching a RABBIT much larger than itself. If you interrupt one, stay perfectly still. It may re-emerge and may even stand on its hind legs in order to have a good look at you.

(34) At the other side of the ridge of Knag Hill, a marker pole points down to the LEFT. At the bottom a stile leads out onto a tarred road, where on exiting you go to the RIGHT.

(35) Once on the road, follow it carefully for the remaining 1ml/1.6km back into Waterville.

If you are passing this way when a dusky summer's evening begins to close in, you will surely be visited by a bat, skimming overhead in search of night-flying insects. Contrary to popular myth, these harmless mammals do not attack humans or try to entangle themselves in your hair, but they do have a very important role to play in keeping the number of insects under control. The PIPISTRELLE, which is the smallest of our bats, can eat up to 3,500 insects in one night. In Ireland, there are seven species of bat altogether, some of which are in danger of extinction. The LESSER HORSESHOE BAT is one such endangered species. Though its largest-known population is in Ireland's southwest, their numbers are in the low thousands and dropping due to loss of roosting sites, which up to now were buildings. Unfortunately modern structures are unsympathetic to their needs.

12 – Derrynane

THE SOUTHWEST OF IRELAND, though well known for its scenery, is only slowly becoming appreciated for the wealth of its natural history, a sad situation that has allowed, and is continuing to allow, very valuable national assets to become irretrievably lost. Over a quarter of all rare Irish plants are found here and its profusion of animal life is second to none. Furthermore, the diversity of habitats in county Kerry is so great that practically all the common species of Irish flora and fauna can be encountered within a short distance of one another.

Several reasons exist to explain this largesse of mother nature. Geographically, Kerry's mountainous peninsulas probe far out into the western Atlantic and this gives the region an intensely maritime character. Furthermore, the southwest is the most far-flung periphery of the Eurasian landmass, and is continually bathed in the warming currents of the North Atlantic drift. This ensures that winter temperatures are never too severe and also that summers are never too dry. Consequently, such a wealth and a luxuriance of vegetation occurs that at times it is almost sub-tropical. So, simultaneously, Kerry is forest and bog, mountain and sea, rocky heath and coastal dune, a variable and rich paradise of wilderness that is hard to match anywhere else on the island. And no better place exists to illustrate this unique mix than at the very end of the Iveragh peninsula, along the shores of Derrynane Bay.

WALK DESCRIPTION

LOCATION: The walk begins amid the sand dunes of Derrynane National Park, next to the historic home of Daniel O'Connell, the famous nineteenth-century Irish Liberator. Having travelled the Ring of Kerry road through either Waterville or Sneem, take the road to the beach at the small village of Caherdaniel. Travel 1ml/1.5km from the village to a Y-junction with a sign for Derrynane House. Here, go to the LEFT and immediately take another signposted sideroad to the LEFT, that passes beneath a metal barrier and leads to a large car park. DO NOT follow the road up to the house.

TERRAIN: A moderate circular walk that is accessible to all types. The trail crosses beach and dunes, then follows a right-of-way along a coastal Mass path and over a mountain track, to end in the woods of Derrynane. During wet weather, care should be exercised on rocky tracks, which can become rather slippery.

FEATURES: Coastal wildlife on the beach and dunes; sixth-century abbey; old Mass path; heathland wildlife and rare plants; deciduous woodlands; Derrynane House and Gardens.

LENGTH: 5ml/8km.

TIME: 3hrs.

EQUIPMENT: Waterproof walking boots for some muddy paths. Jacket for higher heathland during cool or windy weather.

WHEN TO WALK: Suitable at any time of the year.

WALK OUTLINE

(1) From the end of the main carpark, follow the footpath out onto the back of the Derrynane dunes. Here, you turn LEFT and walk towards the large estuary mudflats.

Completely exposed at low tide, this wide expanse of sand and mud is frequented by a variety of waders, probing for aquatic insects and worms. Besides the ever-present GULLS, watch for the more interesting and less familiar SANDPIPERS, DUNLIN and PLOVERS. Small flocks of RINGED PLOVERS (*Charadrius hiaticula*) are year-round residents and quite easy to see, as they are tolerant of human presence. Generally brownish on the back and white underneath, they have a conspicuous dark band around the neck and orange-coloured legs.

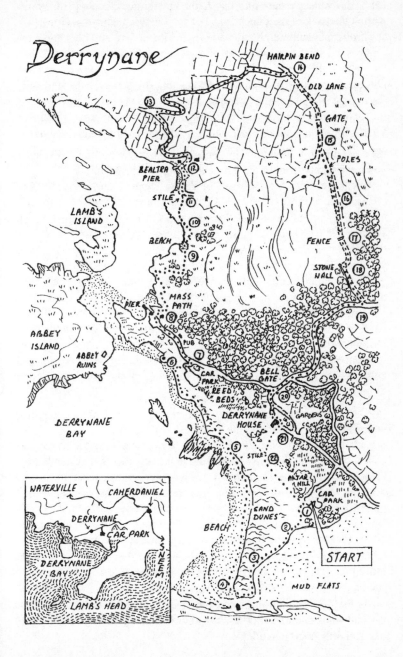

(**2**) At the estuary's shoreline, turn to the RIGHT and walk along the grassy path at the back of the dunes.

Throughout summer, many varieties of flowers are in bloom about the grassy sand meadows, as they are well-sheltered from wave action. This is the more stable fixed section of the dune habitat and is known as Grey Dunes. Common plants like DAISIES and BUTTERCUPS are readily distinguished, but it is the rarer members, such as the yellow-petalled SEA PANSIES (*Viola curtisii*) and the orange-yellow flower tufts of KIDNEY VETCH (*Anthyllis vulneraria*), that make the dunes unique as a habitat.

(**3**) Continue to follow the wire fence that skirts the mudflats, as it leads you towards the front of the dunes and out onto the beach.

As you approach the less fixed, or Yellow Dune system, the vegetation changes noticeably to the dominant MARRAM GRASS (*Ammophila arenaria*), a prime agent in the dune system's formation. Amongst the tall stands of this coarse and spiky grass, PURPLE ORCHIDS and SEA HOLLY (*Eryngium maritimum)* grow. About your feet great numbers of empty SNAIL shells are to be found, their large numbers due to the rich supplies of calcium available in the sand for shell-making. GRASSHOPPERS whirr on balmy sunny days, while above your head the singing SKYLARKS vie to out-sing the MEADOW PIPITS. Dunes host an incredible variety of species, but they are extremely delicate wildlife areas and suffer significantly from excessive trampling, and worse, motorcycle scramblers. Such pressures result in blowouts of the hills by the wind, and thus begins the erosion and collapse of the dunes. Therefore, I have purposely avoided crossing through them.

(**4**) Once on the beach, turn to the RIGHT and walk along its entire length to where the rocks jut out into the water.

Rather empty of life on first sight, the sea has in fact a greater concentration and diversity of wildlife in it than any other system on the planet. Beneath the sand, numerous burrowing creatures wait to emerge with the returning tide, some, such as BRISTLE WORMS, betraying their presence by throwing up heaped sand casts at the opening to their tunnels. Only an occasional hint of the presence of larger creatures reaches us, when, for instance, the tide ebbs or migration and breeding habits bring them close to the shore. Unfortunately, we are now likely to encounter birds polluted by oil, and DOLPHINS and WHALES drowned by being accidentally snared in discarded fishing nets or choked by the vast amount of plastic that we all must accept responsibility for. Our twentieth-century waste is increasingly clogging up and hastening the death of the oceans and you will not fail to miss it scattered about the beach.

Common residents of tidal rock pools, anemones have a ring of stinging
tentacles for protection, while the hermit crab takes up permanent
residence in an empty whelk shell to
aid camouflage.

NOTE: During stormy weather and the high spring tides around March 21
and September 21, you may have to walk along the top of the dunes.

(5) Pass the rocks, walk up onto the top of the sandy embankment and
continue STRAIGHT AHEAD, parallel to the beach.

Amidst the rocks, small pools offer an even better glimpse of the rich
coastal wildlife. Living on the edge of two worlds, twixt the land and the
sea, the various organisms of the seashore have had to adapt to the most
extreme conditions. Twice daily submerged in salty water and twice daily
exposed to dry air, with the odd splash of rainwater thrown in, these
inhabitants have developed unique lifestyles controlled by the rising and
falling of the tides. Hidden by day or during low tide, numerous small
creatures remain perfectly camouflaged beneath the seaweeds and rock
crevices. Others adopt protective measures – the HERMIT CRAB, for
example, squeezes its body into the empty shell of a DOG WHELK, which it
drags around after itself.

(6) At the end of the beach, where the timber holiday home sits atop the
rock, go to the RIGHT and onto the car park road. Turn LEFT and continue up
to the main road.

(7) On reaching the main road turn to the LEFT and follow the sign for
Derrynane Abbey down to the road's end at the car park of Derrynane pier.

Across the dunes on the left of the car park is Abbey Island. This tenth-century ruin is associated with the seventh-century St Finian, from whom the area gets its name, Derrynane (*Doire Fhionnán*, or 'Finian's oak grove').

(8) At the car park, there is a house on the right, just above the pier. As you approach the house, watch for a few stone steps in the low stone wall on your RIGHT. This leads you on to the Mass path.

The old Mass path weaves its way in and around the rocks that run down to the seashore. These can be rather slippery in wet weather, thus care needs to be exercised. The path was once a well-used track that connected isolated coastal communities in the days before the car. Today, it retains its natural charm and is a delightful rock garden of wild flowers each summer. Strange exotic plants cram the path sides, but it is the spectacular orange blooms and lance-shaped leaves of MONTBRETIA, in July and August, that are most breathtaking.

(9) Eventually, the path emerges onto a small stony beach. Cross this and find the crudely cut steps in the sloping rocks to the RIGHT of the beach. These will lead you back up onto the path.

When I first wrote this book this little cove was covered in washed-up plastic rubbish. However, some conscientious individual has cleaned up the area. I wish them good health and we can all learn from their good example. If everyone brushed outside their own front door ...

(10) Continue along the path as it wanders through untamed rockeries of HEATHER and GORSE, splashed with rainbows of many different coloured wild flowers from spring to autumn.

If you are lucky, you may discover one of Derrynane's unique treasures and one of Ireland's rarest plants. This is the white-flowered KERRY LILY (*Simethis planifolia*). It grows only in these few acres of coastal heath around Derrynane. Please do not interfere with it in any way, as such a rare

The Kerry lily (*Simethis planifolia*) is a rarity unique to this coastal stretch. Concern for its continued survival should guarantee the area's protection from exploitation.

The style of the traditional Irish farmstead blends in perfectly
with the environment.

plant needs every assistance to save it from extinction. More importantly
though, the presence of this protected plant ensures that no developments
will ever be allowed along this coastal region. Lovers of the wild outdoors
will undoubtedly appreciate the significance of keeping this plant alive
and well.

(11) The path arrives at a stile that steps down onto a track. Follow the
track STRAIGHT ahead, passing along the back of the small beach and out
by some houses to Bealtra pier, and a tarred road.

(12) From the pier take the tarred road to the RIGHT and follow it as it winds
uphill.

As you climb, fine views across the bay unfold. Away on the distant
horizon is the end of the Beara peninsula and off its coast, Dursey Island.
Closer to home is Deenish Island and, behind it, the larger Scariff Island.

(13) Presently the road arrives at a sharp right-hand bend, where a road
branches off to the left. However, continue to follow the road up to the
RIGHT for the next 0.5ml/0.8km until a sharp left-hand hairpin bend is met.

All about the stony hills, small farmsteads exude their rustic and
romantic charm. Amidst the rich trellis of stone-walled fields, farmhouses
with high-chimneyed gables and outhouses of crafted stone are
surrounded by rusty-red haybarns and reeks of turf. Unfortunately, the
sterile architecture of modern holiday homes contrasts bitterly with these
older, more traditional buildings, detracting from the rich culture and
heritage they have unwittingly imposed upon.

(14) On reaching the hairpin bend, a stony track with a cul de sac (a dead end) sign branches off to the RIGHT. Leave the tarred road here and follow the track past the picturesque farmhouse on the right, heading towards the rocky heathland.

(15) Go through a gate (reclose it after you), and watch for a point about 200m further on, where a line of poles leaves the trackside and rises uphill across the heathland. Leave the lane here and follow the poles up across the rough heath on your LEFT, part of the Kerry Way walking route.

(16) Near the top of the hill the old lane begins to reappear as a grass-covered track, half-smothered in BRACKEN and FURZE. Maintain a STRAIGHT course.

On the hilltop, a large rocky outcrop makes an ideal place to picnic and enjoy the view. From April onwards, CUCKOOS (*Cuculus canorus*), newly arrived from Africa, court-call across the rocky hollows. Towards autumn, it is not unusual to spot a TURTLE DOVE (*Streptopelia turtur*). Usually a summer visitor to southern England, it does make a brief appearance in the southwest as a passage migrant *en route* to Central Africa for the winter. In fact, any coastal region is wont to provide unusual sightings of uncommon birds, ranging from BALD-HEADED EAGLES to AMERICAN REDSTARTS.

(17) Following the track, descend on the other side of the hill, where a stone fence, with sheepwire on top, blocks the path. Cross over this and keep on the track.

On the heathland, several abandoned stone crofts can be identified. Quite probably of pre-famine origin, their small size and isolated locations are characteristic of the difficulties that people endured during those harsh times.

(18) After about 164ft/50m the overgrown track swings around to the RIGHT and leads down towards a stone wall. Keep your eyes open. Go to the LEFT at the wall and follow what is little more than a muddy path through the wooded copse.

You have now entered the woods of Derrynane. The varied mix of OAK, HOLLY and many more deciduous trees is rather stunted at this high altitude, but is packed with a variety of small songbirds, whose chorus rings out across the hills in early spring. In particular, listen for the sweet melody of the WILLOW WARBLER (*Phylloscopus trochilus*), a rare summer visitor that inhabits the scrubby woods.

(19) The path reaches a wire fence with a stile and leads onto a tarred road. Go to the RIGHT and follow the road downhill for 0.5ml/0.8km to a Y-junction. Here, turn RIGHT.

Towering BEECH trees and clumps of HAZEL overhang the downward journey. In autumn, the rich colour of their golden leaves is quite spectacular.

(20) At the bottom of the hill and on a bend, you reach the white-washed Bell Gate of Derrynane House on your LEFT, which leads you into the back of the house. Follow the avenue and take the first turn RIGHT towards the main house.

The gate has a bell in its arched pillar which was used to call people back to the house when required. The avenue is flanked by the formal gardens that are now under the care of the Office of Public Works. Along the wall on the left, just inside the gate, clumps of the unique Lusitanian ST PATRICK'S CABBAGE display their starry rosette of leaves and delicate white flowers during July. However, it is the exotic trees and flowers, thriving in the sub-tropical conditions of Derrynane, that really catch your eye. If you explore the gardens thoroughly, you will discover the rare ARBUTUS TREE and, in hidden corners, wondrous FERN trees that give the illusion of a tropical paradise.

(21) Pass by the front of the house and go STRAIGHT, crossing the front lawns and heading towards the beach.

The house and adjacent private church contain fine collections of memorabilia and furniture that once belonged to Daniel O'Connell. There is also a café at the rear of the house if you wish to take a rest.

(22) On the other side of the front lawn, a small footbridge and gate take you across a deep gully and out onto the back of the dunes. Cross the dunes at an angle to the LEFT, keeping to the right of the large rock ahead. This brings you back to the start of the walk at (1). The large rock is known as Altar Hill and provides a good vantage-point to overlook the dunes before you finish the walk.

13 – Rossbeigh

ON THE NORTHERN SIDE of the Iveragh peninsula, mountainous heaths look down upon the wide expanses of sand which choke the upper reaches of Dingle Bay. Of comparatively recent origin, the bay was once a wide swampy plain between the parallel mountain ridges of the present Iveragh and Dingle peninsulas. It, and all other low-lying coastal areas, were drowned by the rise in sea levels that occurred in the aftermath of the last Ice Age, approximately eight thousand years ago. This means that the Iveragh peninsula is really a chain of mountains rising straight out of the sea. Thus, it is hard to walk very far without bumping into a precipitous wall of heath. Scarred and pitted by the movement of mile-high glaciers during the previous two million years, the peninsula's mountainous spine was sculpted into a clutter of cliff-rimmed corries and V-shaped valleys, while vast amounts of eroded silt were washed down to clog up the drowned coastal inlets.

Rossbeigh Hill affords a fine opportunity to view the wave-washed sandy spits that guard the inner reaches of this drowned fiord and the spectacular ridged peaks which run out on either side. Additionally, you get an excellent view of the curtain wall of cragged and cliffed coombes

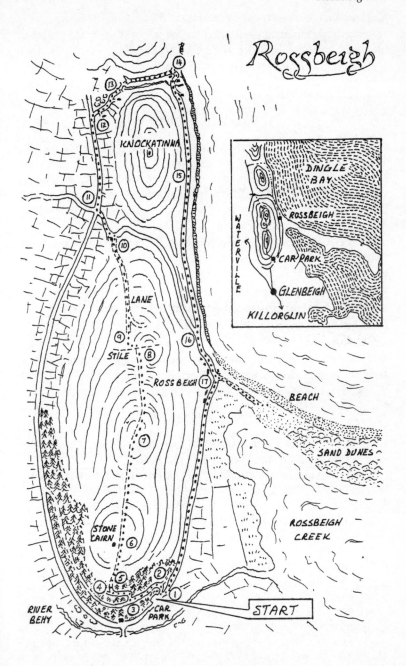

Rossbeigh

that surrounds the network of corrie lakes on the foothills of the nearby Glenbeigh mountain range. Behind this curtain wall layer after layer of mountain folds hide an extensive network of deep glacial valleys. Such regions are practically devoid of human settlement and have, for centuries, been abandoned to a rich and rugged wilderness where nature reigns supreme.

WALK DESCRIPTION

LOCATION: The walk begins amidst the coniferous plantation of Faha Wood. This is adjacent to the village of Glenbeigh, which overlooks Dingle Bay from the northern side of the Iveragh peninsula. At the western end of the village, take the RIGHT turn for Rossbeigh Strand, cross a stone bridge and again, go to the RIGHT. Shortly after, the open car park of Faha Wood is met on the LEFT.

TERRAIN: A moderate circular walk over the rounded dome of Rossbeigh Hill (905ft/275m) and along the narrow green-roads that follow the coastline.

FEATURES: Coniferous woods; upland heath; country green-roads; beach and dunes; fabulous coastal and mountain views; mountaintop cairn.

LENGTH: 5ml/8km.

TIME: 4hrs.

EQUIPMENT: Strong walking shoes; waterproof leggings desirable in wet, showery weather. Binoculars an advantage.

WHEN TO WALK: Suitable at any time of the year.

WALK OUTLINE

(1) From the car park, follow the path through the picnic area and climb the path, by the roadside, that leads up into the woods.

Around the picnic area, copses of SILVER BIRCH trees push up through the rich swards of BRACKEN and WOOD RUSH. These have recolonised the open-lit spaces on the verge of the evergreen plantation. Within the coniferous woods, the ground vegetation quickly vanishes due to the absence of bright sunshine, save for the fungi that appear during October and November. In those parts where the light does penetrate, straggling MOUNTAIN ASH trees poke upwards and the woodland floor supports rich displays of the white-petalled WOOD SORREL (*Oxalis acetosella*), throughout April and May. Here and there, clumps of FROTHEN and FERN survive in dense thickets. Overhead, numerous CHAFFINCHES can usually be spotted weaving through the branches.

(2) Passing through the coniferous woods, the path swings around a bend

Fungi are important decomposers in coniferous woods. In the absence of light-loving plants they account for the principle ground flora beneath the dense shade of the evergreen trees.

to the left and then runs along a straight stretch that gradually climbs uphill.

(**3**) After several hundred metres you must watch very carefully for an indistinct path that branches up through the trees on your RIGHT.

A 'Kerry Way' marker pole stands just beyond the spot at which you leave the more distinct path. If there is a clearing in the trees on your left you should be able to look straight up the main street of Rossbeigh village. However, take note that due to storms in the winter of 2001, many trees have fallen in this section of the wood, making the ascent up to the heathland above the wood very difficult. The path has become lost and until the felled trees are cleared away you must make your way up through the trees as best you can until you break out onto the heathland at the top. As you rise it is best to maintain a gradual diagonal course towards point (4), and then carry on upwards until you reach point (5).

(**4**) Presently the path comes to a Y-junction, and here you go to the RIGHT. You may be able to see the opening at the wood's end above you from this junction. A steep ascent full of BRACKEN fern leads upwards and eventually arrives at a broken stone wall at the top of the wood.

(**5**) Pass out of the wood onto the heath. Here, a wire fence atop a broken stone wall runs upwards through the heather. Keeping this on your left, follow it STRAIGHT AHEAD to the top of the hill.

As you climb, look back over the trees to the village of Glenbeigh, where fine views begin to open up. To the LEFT of the village, the muddy estuary of Castlemaine harbour stretches inland to the top of the bay, sheltered by the long sandy spits of Rossbeigh, Cromane further in, and Inch on the other side as it projects out from the Dingle peninsula. During winter, the bay and its tidal mudflats are an important bird sanctuary, now a fully protected nature reserve.

Looking back to the right and downhill, you may spot the ruined tower of Wynn's folly, a mansion built by Lord Headley of Aghadoe in 1867. This tyrannical landlord evicted so many of the local tenants, and so cruelly, that it became headline news in the London *Times* of the day. Wynn's folly was burnt to the ground during the civil war in 1922.

(**6**) From the top of the first hill, continue STRAIGHT to the next summit, following the well-defined path and keeping next to the wire fence.

At the top of this first hill and on the other side of the fence, is a ruined stone cairn, known as Laghtshee ('fairy monument'), a name derived from the days when people believed that many of these ancient artifacts belonged to the fairies. In fact, it is the remains of an ancient burial mound, probably dating back four thousand years to Neolithic times. Now little more than a heap of stones, it could easily be missed.

(**7**) On reaching the main summit of Rossbeigh Hill (905ft/275m) continue to follow the fence DOWN into the heathered valley, then UP again on the other side to the next rounded peak.

From the main summit, good views are available on your left, across to the rugged wall of mountains, which encircles a clutter of corrie lakes, barely visible in their hollowed-out glaciated coombes. As you make for the next summit, you may encounter a herd of semi-wild GOATS, keeping as great a distance between you and them as they can manage. These were originally domesticated stock, that have since taken to the wild, and so do not represent a true native herd of wild animal. However, you are more likely to encounter the odd wild hare racing across the heath. The Irish MOUNTAIN HARE (*Lepus timidus*) is a distinctive race, an endemic subspecies that is quite different from its European neighbours.

(**8**) At the final summit another fence crosses the path. At the corner formed by the two fences the original stile has collapsed completely, so cross over the wire fence with great care. Do not stand on it and damage it. Once over the fence, walk at a forty-five-degree angle down to the LEFT and locate a rough mountain track.

(9) On reaching the track, go to the RIGHT and follow it STRAIGHT DOWN the other side of the hill.

(10) Eventually the track passes down by a house on your left to a T-junction at a tarred road. Go to the LEFT, following the Kerry Way sign.

(11) Shortly, a crossroads is reached with another Kerry Way marker which points you to the RIGHT. Continue along the hedgerowed road for the next 0.25ml/0.4km, until the second RIGHT turn is met.

(12) At the second right turn, which is untarred, go down to the RIGHT.

The narrow road leads you down through high, overgrown hedgerows where, beyond the gate entrance on the right, the road converts to an earthen track. Along the way, numerous native songbirds can be heard as well as seen. Occasionally, LONG-TAILED TITS (*Aegithalos caudatus*), with their pink plumage and white faces, flit about the shelter of the HAZEL and SALLY scrub. These delightful little birds travel in groups as they search the twigs for insects, and can be heard repeatedly calling to one another in a soft, whispering tone.

Long-tailed tits travel together in small flocks, flitting from one bush to another. They keep in contact through their constant whispering calls to each other.

You are unlikely to spot the probably now extinct sea pea – however you will encounter its more
common cousin (above), the yellow-petalled meadow vetchling,
straggling over the hedgerows in late summer.

(13) Continue past the next house on the right and follow the now
grass-covered track through the thickets of SALLY TREES and BRACKEN
FERN. Presently, you cross a small bridge with a gate and the old
abandoned road follows the stream, taking you downhill towards the sea
(the track will be flooded here after rain).

The sheltered gorge is smothered in thickets of purple HEATHER and
DWARF GORSE, which attract large numbers of nectar-seeking insects in
late summer. On more exposed banks of the mountain stream, large
clumps of ROYAL FERN (*Osmunda regalise)* droop over the rocky pools,
their conspicuous summer foliage, a tall spike, protruding from the central
cluster of fronds. Along the wetter parts of the path, in early summer, you
will encounter the purple flowers of the insect-eating BUTTERWORT.

(14) Near the bottom of the hill and just behind some houses, you reach a
gate. Open and reclose. After this swing clockwise to the RIGHT and walk
UP between the two houses to reach the tarred road.

(15) Walk back along the straight road to reach Rossbeigh beach and
dunes.

Above you on the right, waves of heathland rise steeply upwards. On your left, the sea has eaten deeply into the soft cliff line leaving a jumble of large, discarded rocky boulders at its base. In parts the road has collapsed recently, thus keep well away. You can observe this dangerous cliff safely from the beach. Rather exposed and too close to human habitation for SEALS to be frequent visitors, these waters provide summer fishing for large rafts of black GUILLEMOTS and AUKS. These birds breed on the Blasket Islands, which are visible in the distance at the end of the Dingle peninsula.

(16) Eventually, the road joins another coming down from the hill on your right and this leads you towards the beach, an ideal place for a swim or a rest. At the beach, the long spit of sand dunes extends into the bay, and here a number of extremely rare and delicate plants grow amongst the dune slacks.

A rarity, once unique to the dunes of Rossbeigh, is the SEA PEA (*Lathyrus maritimus*), which grew in extensive carpets about the dunes. Sadly, it has vanished and may now be extinct here. Several other rare species have also vanished from this site, including the extremely rare NATTERJACK TOAD. As a result of the threat that various tourist-related practices pose to the animal and plant life of the dunes, it is advisable to keep to the edge of the dunes or walk along the seashore.

(17) Having visited the beach or dunes, return to the tarred road and go to the LEFT. Pass the small cluster of houses and follow the main road for 1ml/1.6km, back to the car park at the starting point of the walk.

As you walk, you pass the wide tract of mudflats behind the dunes and, in the winter months, you should see plenty of waders, such as the CURLEW, LAPWING, GOLDEN PLOVER, SANDPIPER, STINT and DUNLIN, especially when the tide is out.

14 – Anascaul

WHEN ALONE IN THE MOUNTAINS, you may experience a feeling of detached loneliness that makes you want to rush back to the land of the living and the safety of the social herd. But if you get to know the inhabitants of these bleak landscapes intimately, and learn to understand the complex conditions of their survival, you eventually discover the warmth to be found in their majestic expanses of open terrain.

The moods and tempers of these uncompromising regions vary enormously. On an unyielding day, you can savour the chilling bleakness of the hills in a way that tests you to the very depths of your physical and emotional tolerance. Walk into a deep, precipitous coombe, where the dark cliffs tower upwards to scrape a grey angry sky, while down from the back of a sunless glen, a howling cold wind tears across the surface of a black bottomless tarn. The whipping wind lashes spray into the air and drives it across the naked valley floor to burn the skin on your exposed face. Your bent frame pushes onwards against the wickedness of nature to the monotonous squelching of your water-sodden boots – the only other sounds are the persistent cranking and croaking of a lone raven echoing above the whine of the cutting wind. Enough to make you want to flee

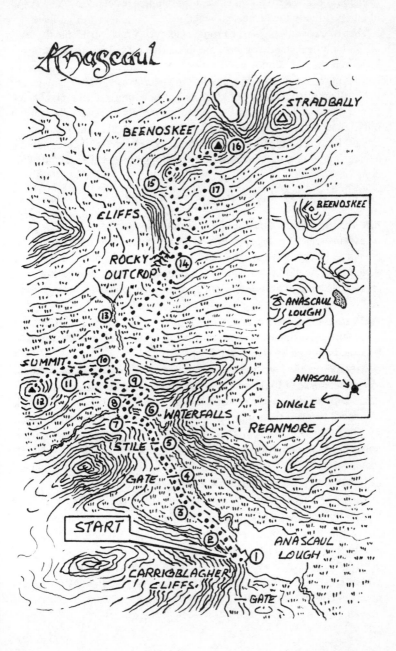

from the godforsaken spot and take up permanent residence by the warmth of an open fire in the nearest crowded pub!

Then there are the days when some old track spirals you up into the arms of the high peaks and you become instantly enthralled. A warming sun kisses the heathery slopes, and a gentle breeze wafts the aromatic scents of a thousand blooms across the timeless heath. Waves of purple and golden hues roll off into an infinity of hidden glens and forgotten summits, which ring to the enchanting sounds of secret waterfalls and cascades spilling into bewitched and hypnotic pools of sparkling water. The heart of the upland lies exposed and wraps its irresistible charm tightly around you. You are gone! Lost to the seas of heath, melting into the hidden land of the wild and free.

WALK DESCRIPTION

LOCATION: Lough Anascaul lies 3ml/4.8km north of the village of Anascaul on the Dingle peninsula. At the western end of Anascaul village, cross the bridge and take the road on the RIGHT, signposted for Loch Abhainn an Scáil (Lough Anascaul). Follow this road, going RIGHT at a crossroads, until two adjoining gates are met at its end. Pass through these and drive down to the lakeside car park.

TERRAIN: A moderate one-way climb along a fine old green-road to the mountain tops. The rough and stony track is quite traversable, but does become boggy and waterlogged in parts.

OPTION: From the high moors you can complete a strenuous climb to the top of Beenoskee Mountain. However, this should be attempted only by those with serious mountain-walking experience, and then only in fine clear weather when there is no risk of mist descending on the upper peaks.

FEATURES: Picturesque Lough Anascaul, in its spectacular, amphitheatred glen; rolling upland heath amidst the peaks of the Dingle mountains; mountain streams and waterfalls; lakeshore flora and fauna.

LENGTH: 4ml/6.5km one-way route. OPTION: 5.5ml/9km.

TIME: 2.5hrs. The OPTION is 5hrs from start to finish.

EQUIPMENT: Strong waterproof walking boots or wellingtons and warm jacket for higher moors. The OPTION will require waterproof leggings during wet weather and proper waterproof mountain boots with a good grip. A compass, and a supply of food and liquid are desirable.

WHEN TO WALK: Suitable at any time of the year, but the OPTION should not be attempted during wet and misty weather, or when there is a risk of low cloud.

WALK OUTLINE

(1) Having parked at the car park overlooking the lough, walk UP the old track that leads into the back of the coombe.

Across the water, the high cliffs of Dromavalla tower upwards like shattered and turreted castles, rising sheer out of steep and unclimbable slopes of scree. On your left, the puckered and equally precipitous Carrigblagher cliffs of Knockmulanane Mountain scream upwards to the roofless sky, where PEREGRINES and RAVENS soar, their warning cries echoing across this wondrous amphitheatre of rock. It was atop the cliffs of Dromavalla that Cúchulainn, a legendary hero who had numerous dealings with women in distress, is believed to have had one of his abodes. One particular lady, Scál ní Mhurnain, asked Cúchulainn to fight a frightful giant for her. Cúchulainn stood on top of Dromavalla, while the giant commanded the top of Knockmulanane. A great battle ensued, each firing boulders at the other. But Cúchulainn was hit and Scál ní Mhurnain, thinking he had been killed, drowned herself in the lake. Hence its name, Lough Anascaul.

(2) On the lakeshore, the presence of fisherpersons testifies to the water's purity. Close observation shows the water to be alive with a myriad of

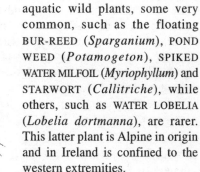

aquatic wild plants, some very common, such as the floating BUR-REED (*Sparganium*), POND WEED (*Potamogeton*), SPIKED WATER MILFOIL (*Myriophyllum*) and STARWORT (*Callitriche*), while others, such as WATER LOBELIA (*Lobelia dortmanna*), are rarer. This latter plant is Alpine in origin and in Ireland is confined to the western extremities.

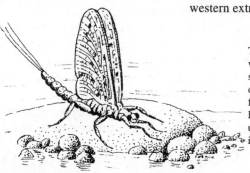

The annual rise of the winged, adult mayfly in early summer is the fisherperson's delight. Metamorphosing from the larval stage at the lake bottom, they draw fish upwards as they try to escape into the air.

The sweet chamomile flowers in July add a vibrant
splash of colour to rough and stony ground.

(3) Leaving the lake behind, the track follows the line of the stream
entering the lake.

In summer, the gentle flow of the crystalline water teems with the
emerging larvae of MAYFLY and CADDISFLY. These spend the bulk of their
lives as grubs at the bottom of the stream, metamorphosing into winged
adults so they can mate and complete their life cycles. Thus they have
remarkably short adult lives. One particular species metamorphoses
without a mouth and so cannot feed, its prime objective being to breed
within its short adult life of twenty-four hours, after which time it dies.
Along the way, watch for the DAMSELFLY which can be seen mating in the
overgrown vegetation of RUSH.

(4) When you reach a rusty iron gateway, pass through it (close it after you)
and follow the line of the old track UPWARDS.

Over to your left is a cluster of deciduous trees, miraculous survivors of
past depravities practised on the land by humans. Up to the seventeenth
century, this whole valley would have been cloaked in aboriginal forest.
Today, constant sheep-grazing has put an end to tree regeneration and
ensures the continued barrenness of the mountains.

(5) Continue UP, passing through another gate using the stepped stile on the
left, after which the track becomes covered in rich swards of short grass.

In the month of July, you find creeping clumps of SWEET CHAMOMILE
(*Chamaemelum nobile*), easy to identify by its beautifully fragrant scent.

Its white-petalled, yellow flowers make a herbal tea that is renowned as a tonic for acidic stomach. But, it is perhaps more commonly associated with Beatrix Potter's book for children, *The Tale of Peter Rabbit*. When Peter Rabbit felt poorly after eating too many of Mr McGregor's lettuces, his mother dosed him with chamomile tea!

(6) Further up, the track gets extremely weather-torn and needs careful manoeuvring.

Across the glen to the right, small waterfalls cascade down through a cliffed gully, their noise drowning out everything else when the mountains pour out their deluge after heavy rain. Storm-torn, the picturesque falls flow into deep pools rimmed with coats of shaggy MOSS and EMPEROR FERNS, the romantic's ideal location for an exhilarating swim in the summer heat.

(7) As you continue UP, another more accessible river is heard, rushing down the gully beneath you on the right. This is the Garrivagh river. Spilling over the raw rocks in sparkling sheets of spray, the white foaming streaks of water splash into mirrored pools and send haunting and echoing sounds vibrating across the glens. These pocket oases of the uplands retain the original, though now impoverished, vegetation that once dominated the hills. Canopied in cooling shade by overhanging trees of ASH, the crannied walls of the rocky pools are decked in a myriad of plants such as GOLDEN ROD (*Solidage virgaurea*), ST PATRICK'S CABBAGE (*Saxifraga spatularis*) and BUTTERWORT (*Pinguicula grandiflora*).

(8) The track crosses a small bridge with some sheep wire, and continues upward by a zigzag route.

As you climb, excellent views of the glaciated valley open out below and the lake comes back into sight, while on the distant horizon, the peaks of the Macgillycuddy's Reeks are visible on a clear day.

(9) Later a second, and then a third, bridge is crossed, beneath which a small stream runs down over slippery sheets of rock. Around its sides are rich growths of the insect-eating SUNDEW and BUTTERWORT, the latter considered by many to be one of Ireland's most beautiful flowers. Whether this is true or not, its ability to eat insects makes it one of Ireland's more fascinating plants. A true survivor in the poorly nourishing soils of the bogs!

(10) Further on, the laneway becomes very muddy and waterlogged and choked with dense thickets of RUSH. It is hard to traverse without the proper footwear, but provides the perfect location for the LESSER SPEARWORT (*Rannunculus flammula*) to flourish. This member of the buttercup family is recognised by its yellow flowers in summer. In early spring on the surrounding moors, the vegetation is rather sparse, as it is composed mostly of mountain grasses, like the PURPLE MOOR GRASS (*Molinia*) with little or no HEATHER. However, come May, white blobs of BOG COTTON (*Eriophorum angustifolium*) stretch across the moors in billowing sheets of white, heralding the arrival of summer.

(11) STOP when the old road reaches the summit where the high bog stretches across to the distant slope of Beenoskee Mountain (2713ft/820m). Leave the track here and go to the LEFT for a few hundred metres to reach the rise (1200ft/360m), which is covered in grass and rocks. The track itself wanders off into the distant heath, where eventually it disappears amidst the waves of PURPLE MOOR GRASS.

(12) If doing the OPTION, see (12) below. From the small rise, you can fully appreciate the expanse that spreads out around you – an endless and magnificent wilderness that runs off in all directions. Surrounded by the many peaks of the peninsula's mountains, the high moors appear to be untainted by the hand of man. There is more wilderness than fertile farmland on the Dingle peninsula, which, though of little commercial worth, is of enormous value to the large reservoirs of wildlife it supports. Looking northeast with your back to Anascaul, the rounded dome of Beenoskee looms over the valley, which continues down and out to the other side of this mountainous spine. The old track goes on through the valley towards Clochan beach, which can be glimpsed in the distance. In the days before the motor car, farmers used this track as a short cut when travelling with their cattle. To the left are the steep-pocketed slopes of Mount Brandon, Ireland's second-highest peak.

(1) Return by the same route to the car park.

OPTION

This requires a certain amount of experience of crossing upland heath and you will need to use the map frequently. In these areas of high cliffs and descending mists, there is usually only one way up and one way down and you MUST NOT deviate from it. There is no road or path to follow and you need to be able to recognise the signs of danger that are part and parcel of the uplands.

(12) Leaving the rise, head due east back across the track, and traverse the wet and soggy rise of blanket bog, making for the lower, RIGHT-hand side of the peak visible in the distance. Then begin the ascent up towards a pyramidal outcrop of rocks that is visible halfway up the slope. The way is rough, boggy and, at times, dips in and out of hollows with squelching clumps of SPHAGNUM MOSS. In days of old, this dried moss was used to dress wounds. Other plants are also to be found, such as purple HEATHER and LING, but the dominant plant up here, in the dense thickets, is PURPLE MOOR GRASS. A walk through this in summer will coat your legs in the white froth of CUCKOO SPITS, the protective larval cases of FROGHOPPER (*Cercopidae*) insects, with their unusual frog-shaped heads.

(13) At the other side of the bog, the ground dips down to a small stream, half hidden in the heath. Crossing this, the ground becomes much drier as it begins to rise up the steeper slope, up towards the pyramidal outcrop now on your LEFT.

The thickets of HEATHER persist all the way up and progress is slow. If it has been raining, leggings are essential at this point. Several insects abound in summer and you may spot the LARGE HEATH BUTTERFLY (*Coenonympha tuillia*), which is usually confined to the heathlands, where it gets plenty of COTTON GRASS, the plant food it requires.

(14) A rest on reaching the pyramidal outcrop allows one to survey the spectacular scenery still unfolding. Looking southwards to the long spine of Reamore, just above Lough Anascaul, you may be able to see numerous stones crowning the top, many arranged in an unusual line along its spine. Their function is unknown. In the centre is a large pile of stones called Cúchulainn's House. However, its association with this mythical Celtic hero is probably misleading, as he doesn't appear in legends until 100 BC – at least a thousand years after the cairn was erected. It is more likely to be an old burial mound, its central chamber having collapsed inwards. Such structures are found on a number of high mountaintops, and are associated with the Bronze Age settlers who erected the standing stones and ring forts that occur all over the farmland below. A person of great nobility would have been buried in this elevated spot, to highlight their importance among the tribes that colonised the area roughly 3500 years ago.

(15) Continue to climb up towards the false peak visible ahead, avoiding the rocky cliffs on your left. The ground becomes stonier as you climb and at times nothing more then sheets of moss cover the slope. Ultimately the upper, boulder-strewn peak is reached and here you discover that the true peak, at 826m, is still higher again and further to your RIGHT.

From this lower peak there are excellent views down over the other side of the peninsula, with the wide expanse of Brandon Bay to the left and Tralee Bay to the right, separated by the expansive spit of the Magharees peninsula protruding out onto the sea. Further north, the coast of Clare is visible, and on a clear day the Cliffs of Moher are discernible.

The cormorant, wings outstretched to dry, is a familiar sight about our lakes.

(16) A vast pile of boulder scree leads across the flat ridge and ultimately up onto the true peak of Beenoskee, which looks very much like an enormous Iron Age burial mound.

Dangerous cliffs plummet down from the northern side of Beenoskee into the waters of Lough Choimin, a glacial corrie lake that separates you from the opposite peak of Stradbally Mountain. Further east along the spine of the Dingle peninsula, the next conspicuous high peak is Caher Conree (835m). Looking south, the waters of Dingle Bay are now visible, beyond which lies the expansive range of mountains that make up the Iveragh peninsula. The high peaks on the left are those of the Reeks and Ireland's highest mountain, Carrauntoohil, at 1039m.

(17) Leaving the peak, descend diagonally to the pyramidal outcrop encountered at (14) on the way up, taking care as you descend as it is steep and boulder-strewn.

(14) From the pyramidal, rocky outcrop, continue to drop down to the lower slopes, avoiding the blanket bog crossed on the way up from point (12) by dropping down below it. Once you are below the rise of the blanket bog, swing to the RIGHT, cross the top of the valley and work your way onto the old track near point (11).

The way is still wet and soft, so proceed slowly. Also avoid descending onto the track too soon, as the slope is too steep and such a short cut may prove more dangerous in the long run.

(2) Returning to the walk's end by the lake of Anascaul, RAVENS kite and glide about above the high cliffs of Reamore on the left and Carrigblagher cliffs on your right.

Thickets of RUSH and YELLOW FLAG (*Iris pseudacorus*) rim the shoreline here and you may flush out a SNIPE or two. Out on the water, CORMORANTS stand like sentries on the offshore rocks. These unusual birds dive for fish and, on returning to their rocky perches, have to hold their wings up to dry because they lack the usual coating of water-repellent oil on their feathers which all modern-day birds possess. This very primitive feature identifies the species as an ancient stock, relatively unchanged from the Jurassic period – over 150 million years ago – when birds were evolving from reptiles. In fact, these divers are the third-oldest-known bird type in the world today, possessing the real teeth and bony tail that link ancient dinosaurs with modern birds. They are a living fossil!

15 – Ballydavid Head

THE ROCKS OF KERRY are as old as life itself. The grains of sand that went to form the initial bedrock were laid down as sedimentary layers in an ancient sea at the same time as the first sparks of life were beginning to emerge over six hundred million years ago. Then, four hundred million years ago, an explosive volcanic period erupted, pushing the seabed above water as a land of high relief, splattered with numerous laval flows. The fledgling Ireland had been born.

In time, the elements wore down the mountains, redepositing them as fine-grained sands on a desert floor and giving rise to the present material of our mountains, old red sandstone. However, the original laval flows resisted weathering in parts, and now form the oldest rocks in Kerry. About three hundred million years ago, Ireland sank beneath the sea again for a brief period. Aquatic life filled the sea and the shelled remains of countless marine creatures coated what had once been valleys with a deep layer of white limestone.

Ireland re-emerged from the sea when another series of earth movements occurred 250 million years ago. At the same time, these movements buckled the southwest of Ireland into a series of corrugated folds, pushing the old red sandstone and its 'icing' of limestone into the series of parallel ridges that forms the major mountain chains of present-day Kerry.

Time and exposure to the elements has worn away the limestone coating and reduced these mountains down to their present size, while the Ice Age, in comparatively recent times, has sculpted the Kerry landscape into the many remarkable features it now possesses.

So, written on the landscape is the story of time itself, a story visible throughout the whole of Kerry. And where better to start to discover it than at the beginning, where the volcanic rocks, formed over four hundred million years ago, are solidly beneath your feet as you walk along the tip of the Dingle peninsula.

WALK DESCRIPTION

LOCATION: The walk starts in the village of Feohanagh, 7ml/11km north of Dingle town and situated on the shores of Smerwick harbour, beneath the shadow of Brandon Mountain. On arrival, locate the obvious Y-junction in the centre of the village. There is ample parking in the large open space by the pub called *An Cuinne*.

TERRAIN: A moderate circular walk that follows an ill-defined path along the cliffed coastline as it rises over and around the heather-clad slopes of the headland. It is suitable for those who are reasonably fit. However, due to the precipitous nature of the higher cliffs (830ft/250m) you should exercise caution and not attempt the walk in wild windy weather or when there is a risk of low cloud descending on the upper peaks.

OPTION: You can shorten the walk by skipping the climb up to the cliffs of Beenmore towards the end of the walk.

FEATURES: Heathland wildlife; coastal plant and bird life; early nineteenth-century signal tower; stunning cliffs; impressive views of sea and mountain; ringfort.

LENGTH: 5ml/8km.

TIME: 3hrs.

EQUIPMENT: Walking boots with good grip, waterproof leggings if it has been raining.

WHEN TO WALK: Any time of the year, but best avoided during wild stormy weather and low cloud when the high cliffs are extremely dangerous.

WALK OUTLINE

(1) Having parked at the open space in the centre of the Y-junction, stand with the public house at your back and take the tarred road that goes to the RIGHT towards the distant ridge crowned with a ruined tower.

As you walk, extensive beds of REED (*Phragmites*) border the roadside.

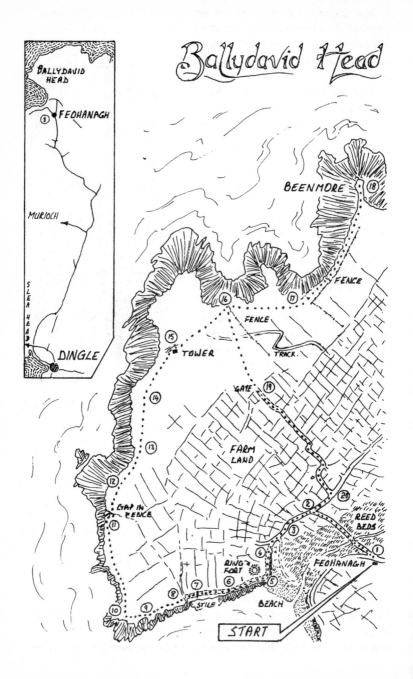

Ballydavid Head

BALLYDAVID HEAD

FEOHANAGH

MURIOCH

SLEA HEAD

DINGLE

BEENMORE

18

FENCE

16

17

FENCE

15

TOWER

TRACK

GATE

19

14

FARM LAND

13

12

GAP IN FENCE

11

2

20

REED BEDS

3

1

4

FEOHANAGH

RING FORT

7

6

5

8

A STILE

BEACH

10

9

START

In late August, when they are at the zenith of their height, they can grow to 9ft/3m. Then, the clambering tendrils of the wild WOODBINE (*Calysteiga sepium*) curl up along their stems, dressing the roadside verge in a clutter of white trumpets.

Soon, you cross the bridge over the Feohanagh river, and gain better views into the depths of the swampy thickets. In early summer, the dry stems of last year's growth provide shelter and nesting sites for several REED BUNTINGS (*Emberiza schoeniculus*) and these are regularly seen flitting from the reeds to the roadside telephone wires.

(2) On arriving at the T-junction take the road to the LEFT.

Below you, the REED beds stretch to the seashore, where a greater mixture of YELLOW FLAG (*Iris pseudacorus*) and GREAT REEDMACE (*Typha latifolia*) can be seen. The attractive golden-yellow flowers of YELLOW FLAG are most eye-catching in early June, when they stand out like bright blobs of sunshine against the duller faded stems of the reeds.

Bindweed and bunting. Reeds not only provide cover for the reed bunting but also provide support for climbing plants like these large bindweed flowers.

(3) As you follow the roadway towards the sea, notice the overgrown stone ditches which are smothered in a variety of wild flowers throughout the summer months, with HONEYSUCKLE, BUTTERCUP and STITCHWORT in the early months of April and May; FOXGLOVE, FUMITORY and WILD DOG ROSE running through June and July; and THISTLE, KNAPWEED and SHEEP'S BIT carrying through to the months of August and September.

(4) Having passed an entrance track to the beach on your left, the road swings uphill to the right. Near here, watch for and take the grassy track on the LEFT. This has a gully with a stream at its entrance, which will have to be jumped. Follow the path along the low cliff that looks down on the beach. The cliff edge crumbles in parts, so do use your common sense.

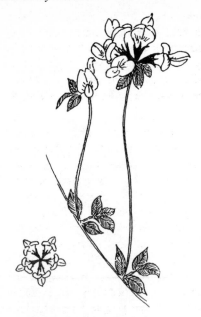

Birds' foot trefoil is one of the many striking and colourful plants that smother the heathery cliffs.

Continue along the path, keeping an eye on the beach and the sea for bird life. HERONS stalk the shoreline rockpools, while CURLEWS and GULLS frequent the beach. Out on the surf, several species of DUCK occur and these increase in numbers come the autumn migrations. Watch for MALLARD, SCOTERS, and the rarer GOOSANDER.

(5) At a bend in the track that swings around to the right, you may notice the remains of an old earthen fort in the field just inside the wall. This was probably the home of a fishing family, dating from the earliest days of recorded history. On the other side of the bay is the mast of Raidio na Gaeltachta, the national radio station which broadcasts in Irish. The station plays a significant part in keeping our native Irish language alive, not only in Ballydavid where it is still the preferred spoken tongue, but throughout the entire country.

(6) As you continue along the coastal path, you can hardly fail to notice what a unique and incredibly rich wildflower garden this is, tended not by human hand but by mother nature herself. The earthen and stone wall on the right is covered with clumps of wild THYME (*Thymus drucei*) and pin-cushion tufts of SEA PINK (*Armeria maritima*), the latter pouring across the path and over the cliffs in stunning sheets of pink blossoms from spring to autumn. Among the many plants visible are VETCH, CLOVER, TREFOIL, DOG VIOLET, YARROW, SILVERWEED, SHEEP'S BIT, GOLDEN ROD, PRIMROSE and STORK'S BILL, all dominating throughout the summer months. Their profusion of colour is matched, if not eclipsed, by the swarms of butterflies that feed upon the nectar-laden blooms. TORTOISE SHELLS, PEACOCKS and PAINTED LADIES are fairly numerous during warm spells. Sadly, the small and delicate COMMON BLUE BUTTERFLIES

(*Polyommatus icarus*) are becoming unique to these isolated coastal heaths because of their loss of habitat to modern intensive farming. Curiously, wherever these blue butterflies frequent, ANTS too may be found. These seek out the butterfly larva and milk a special gland on its back, which exudes a sweet honey-like liquid that the ants cherish. In fact, the ants will even carry the larvae to their required food plants in the vicinity of the ant hill.

(7) The path eventually reaches a wire fence with a crude gate. Pass through, reclosing the gate, then ford the adjacent gully (usually dry) and continue STRAIGHT into the open heath, full of DWARF GORSE (*Ulex gallii*).

This short gorse is native to Ireland and is particularly common in the southwest. It is distinguishable from the taller, and more rampant, introduced variety by the fact that it does not produce its brilliant yellow flowers until autumn. Then, along with the flaming reds of HEATHER, it sets the moors ablaze with colour. The much taller COMMON FURZE (*Ulex europaeus*) flowers in spring and is found throughout the country. It is a particularly persistent weed that can smother large tracts of land, and so it is set ablaze annually to keep it under control. Though it is against the law to burn gorse between April 16 and the following September, these legal guidelines are rarely, if ever, observed and huge mountain fires occur throughout the summer. At times, these are so extensive you might mistake Ireland for a land of volcanoes. Not alone do these fires destroy much of our natural vegetation, but, more importantly, they occur within the breeding season of many birds and butterflies, causing irreparable damage to already diminished breeding stocks. The irony is that earlier in this century, farmers imported the seeds and actually planted the furze! They used it as a remedial food plant for horses during the winter, when little else was available.

(8) Crossing the heath, the path is less distinct. But this should not pose a problem as you will be following the indented and low cliffline out to the end of the headland STRAIGHT AHEAD. Just be sensible and stay in the heath, rather than following the cliffline slavishly, as you would go in and out like a yo-yo.

As you walk, clumps of CROSS-LEAVED HEATH and CREEPING WILLOW become apparent amongst the FURZE. Nearer the cliffs, you may spot the numerous ROCK PIPITS. These are small brown birds, which feed entirely in the inter-tidal zone, leading very different lives from their almost identically dressed cousins, the MEADOW PIPITS.

(9) On reaching the end of the low headland swing to the RIGHT, following the coastline up to the higher and ever-rising cliffs until you meet a wire fence.

All around you, buttresses of rock probe the lashing waves, their crowns covered in thin lawns of grass, manicured to perfection by the SHEEP. However, the tufts of SEA PINK are as plentiful as ever, as sheep dislike their acrid taste. Additionally, despite the area's exposure to a roaring sea, vivid and colourful splashes of green lichen dress the rocks and testify to the purity of the sea air, and to the resilience of these miniature plants in surviving such harsh conditions. In parts, you may notice the unusual nature of the cliffed rocks. These are volcanic in origin and are some of the oldest rocks in Kerry, dating from the Silurian period, 450 million years ago. They are composed entirely of volcanic ash and can be seen not only here, but also on the islands of Inishtooskert, Inishvickillane, Beginish, the northern side of the Great Blasket Island, and at Clogher Head.

(10) Continue to climb up the steep slope until you reach the wire fence. Near the stone wall, look for and use the crude gap, tied with some rope. Open and reclose. Please do not climb over the wire. Passing through the rather awkward stile, continue in a STRAIGHT line towards the hilltop, rather than along the cliffs.

As you climb upwards, the cliffs become more and more spell-binding, dropping in dizzy heights of twisted and beaten folds of rock, caused by their exposure to the onslaught of the ever-pounding waves. Looking across the wide mouth of the bay, you see the conspicuous cliffed peaks of the Three Sisters clearly on the other side. At one time, they were joined to the cliffline on this side to form a continuous land barrier, but this was eventually penetrated by the sea.

(11) The approach to this first summit is heavily littered with stones streaked with white lines of quartz, a form of crystalline silica or sand. The thin layer of peat is almost non-existent in parts, having been removed by turf-cutting. The short stone walls here and there were once used for stacking the fuel against in order to dry it.

The ruined tower atop Ballydavid Head draws one enticingly to the peak.

(12) Following the cliffline, you soon arrive at another series of precipitous cliffs that line the edge in sliding blankets of grassy turf. Beneath, brainless SHEEP forage, oblivious to the fate that awaits them should they make the slightest false move! One slip here and you will roll and tumble down the slippery slopes to a crashing ocean surf from which there is no return. FULMARS slice the air and RAVENS scream from pinnacled rocks as they survey their unchallenged domain.

(13) A little further on, the real summit comes into view, crowned with the jagged machicolations of rock and tower. Walk in a STRAIGHT line across the heath towards this.

As you walk, watch for the few bird species that do manage to eke out a living in these exposed upland heaths. The black CHOUGH occurs at all times of the year, feeding on the coastal meadows and heaths. Though it is declining on the European mainland, it still breeds in large numbers along the west coast of Ireland.

(14) From the tower, walk STRAIGHT AHEAD, but gradually descend into the valley on the RIGHT until a sheepwire fence is met near the cliff edge.

The old signal tower sits just below the summit's apex and so is well sheltered by the rocks on its seaward side. Protected by a screen wall and built of hand-cut stone, mined from the surrounding rocks and then weather-slated, the tower was fully shielded from the elements. It was built by the British at the beginning of the nineteenth century as an observation post against the threat of a French invasion by Napoleon. However, this never occurred and the tower has since deteriorated into a crumbling and ruined state.

(15) If you do not wish to go any further and prefer to avoid the very high cliffs ahead, especially if you have small children with you, shorten the walk by skipping the climb up to Beenmore and returning to the start of the walk. To do this descend the heather-clad slope to the road, visible amongst the farm buildings below, and pick up the walk again at (18). As of 2001, ignore the earthen track that has been cut into the hillside. Instead cross it and source the ancient, stone-walled lane at the bottom of the heath.

OPTION

On reaching the wire fence at (15), cross over it carefully and proceed with caution towards the summit of Beenmore.

The view towards Beenmore is impressive and shows its seaward side to be guarded by spectacular and plummeting cliffs. In some parts, they are dressed in extensive sheets of BRACKEN FERN that pour down to the thunderous applause of a roaring surf, while, in others, they are cracked by recent cliff falls, which expose their ancient sedimentary layers illustrating the buckling pressure that pushed them into the peaks they are today.

(16) Presently, another wire fence is reached that runs parallel to the cliffline. Keep it on your right-hand side and follow it all the way to the top of Beenmore.

(17) From the peak of Beenmore, stunning views may be had of the impressive coastline. Looking back the way you came, the distant shape of the Three Sisters is discernible, while further out to the west the Blasket Islands can be seen. Towards Brandon Mountain the precipitous nature of the cliffed coastline continues indefinitely. Smashed and broken, these towering walls collapse during fierce Atlantic gales, crashing down several hundred feet. Perched up here on a fine summer's day, you are in the ideal place to scan the ocean for GANNETS. Constantly puncturing the ocean surf in search of fish, they drop from heights of 130ft/40m and more. Additionally, many migrants will pass by here on their way south for the winter. Watch for SKUAS, SABINE'S GULLS and SHEARWATERS, all of which make the occasional appearance during their autumn migrations.

(15) Retrace your steps back to the first of the wire fences you encountered on the way to Beenmore. From here, go at an angle to the LEFT, descending across the heath towards the green fields to a laneway that exits between them.

(18) Having reached the laneway, you will find a delicate iron gate bars the way. Open the gate, reclose it and continue down the lane to reach the tarred road by the farmhouses. Follow this to a T-junction.

Strong stone walls guard the way back down, covered, in parts, by drooping clumps of FUCHSIA. Through the interwoven branches, straggling strands of BRAMBLE and HONEYSUCKLE attract the nectar-seeking BEES and WASPS, whose loud drone echoes about the stone walls in a sleepy summer haziness. In the stillness, a WREN flits through the foliage, occasionally uttering notes of disapproval at the human intrusion.

(19) At the T-junction go to the RIGHT and continue until you reach another junction.

(2) You are now back at the first junction of the outward journey. Here, go to the LEFT, and continue back to the car park at (1).

16 – Great Blasket Island

AN ISLAND WALK has a unique charm – that feeling, perhaps, of being far removed from the ordinary toil of your daily existence. Cut off from the outside world, life and time develop their own pace, and you find yourself settling into low gear. With nowhere very far to go and all day to get there, you quickly gravitate into a contentedness with yourself and the here and now. And where better to experience this than on the furthest extremity of the Eurasian landmass, the enchanting Blasket Islands. On a fine summer's day, to walk barefoot across the wind-shaven heath is as close as you can get to peeping into heaven. Surrounded on all sides by a white-foamed, ice-blue sea, and with a balmy sky of muted clouds rolling off into infinity, you feel the distant mountains of the mainland are far away and unreal.

However, a short visit to the Blaskets, though full of romance, disguises the true hardship of having to survive daily on that thin line where two worlds collide, between the mainland and the deep blue sea. During winter gales, coastal islands experience the elements of wind and water at their most violent. Whether it be human or wild beast, the demands placed upon each creature test to the utmost degree. Those that can, adapt, the rest fail and die. The story of the Blasket Islands is thus very much the story of a battle between life and the elements.

Scattered about its naked landscape, the remains of successive waves of human migration lie in ruins, all having eventually surrendered to the isolation and back-breaking hardship. No bush or tree, and none of the larger mainland animals, lives on the island's bleak and shelterless back, apart from the ubiquitous burrowing rabbit. Thus, the real masters of these far-flung islands are the birds of the air and the creatures of the sea. Free from the predations of larger land mammals, including humans, they have learned to use isolation as a tool rather than an enemy in their struggle to survive. Birds breed in enormous numbers on the cliffs and steep sea crags, conferring on these wave-lashed rocks the privilege of being one of the prime breeding areas in Western Europe for many sea birds.

WALK DESCRIPTION

LOCATION: Situated off the very tip of the Dingle peninsula, Great Blasket Island is accessible only in fine weather. During the summer months, the ferry for the island leaves Dunquin pier regularly from about 10am onwards, when the weather is suitable. The pier is 8ml/13km from Dingle on the Slea Head road, and, from the nearby village of Dunquin, is well signposted.

TERRAIN: A delightful circular walk around the steep, cliff-rimmed and heather-clad hills of the mountainous island. The route follows the outline of the old roads and well-defined paths. Suitable for all – if you don't mind the half-hour sea journey in an open boat. However, do exercise considerable caution when walking near the perilously high cliffs, and watch children at all times.

FEATURES: Abandoned settlement of the Blasket islanders; heathland wildlife; sea birds; stone promontory forts, stunning views of the island archipelago.

LENGTH: 4ml/6.5km.

TIME: 2–2.5hrs. The actual walk takes 2–2.5hrs, but the boat journey takes about 0.5hrs each way – and you may also have to wait for a short period before catching the return boat. Therefore, plan on spending a minimum of 5hrs, if not the whole day on the island. You won't regret it!

EQUIPMENT: The ferry usually operates only when the sea is reasonably calm. The return fare (1991 prices) will be about £8 per person. During misty or foggy weather, take a raincoat and waterproof boots. In fine weather, you will be able to travel light and walk the grassy green-roads in light shoes or even barefoot. However, do carry a supply of food.

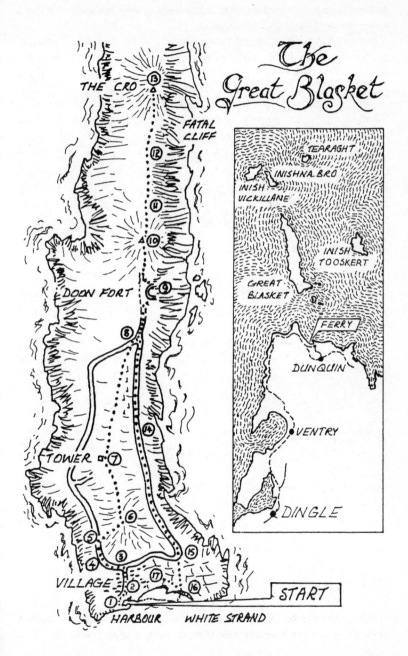

The Great Blasket

THE CRO
FATAL CLIFF
DOON FORT
TOWER
VILLAGE
HARBOUR   WHITE STRAND

TEARAGHT
INISHNA BRO
INISH VICKILLANE
INISH TOOSKERT
GREAT BLASKET
FERRY
DUNQUIN
VENTRY
DINGLE

START

WHEN TO WALK: The island is at its best on a sun-kissed summer's day.
NOTE: Boats are taken at your own risk.

WALK OUTLINE

(1) On arriving at the island's small pier, walk up to the decaying village and turn to the LEFT, passing STRAIGHT through the derelict stone buildings to reach the old road.

This abandoned village once housed a community of people that will be a part of Irish literature forever. For generations, the islanders fought the elements and survived, their lives inseparably bound to the nature of the island. Living off the sea and what they could produce themselves, they maintained a subsistence existence for several generations. Isolated on this tiny, far-flung island, they remained unsullied by the outside world. Their close-knit community retained the fabric of a much older society, keeping alive its ancient language and rich traditions. It was not until 1953 that they abandoned the island for a less harsh life on the mainland.

(2) Now covered in a carpeted sward of short grass, the old road leads you to the top of the village. Walking upwards, you pass the decaying houses of now-scattered families. Out of the lonesome shadows the many stories enacted here still echo. Many of the islanders, seeing their way of life begin to disappear, put their lives and those of their neighbours into print, as in the heart-felt writings of Peig Sayers, Muiris Ó Súilleabháin, Tomás Ó Críomhtháin and others.

After a few hundred metres, you pass a number of houses on your right, with a path between them. The lowest and smallest house has a tarred canvas roof, a small window and a little door that faces uphill. This was the house of the island's king (*teach an rí*) and has since been restored as a small holiday retreat. Behind the king's house are a number of taller houses, still intact, the first of which was the home of Peig Sayers.

(3) Leaving the village behind you, you soon come to a Y-junction. Turn to the LEFT and follow the road upwards.

The grassy track rises steeply, its borders festooned with the yellow heads of TORMENTIL from June to September. As you climb, the village shows itself to have been well situated. The broad girth of the island's hills at its back protects it from the direct effects of ocean gales, while in front is the stunning vista of the mountainous mainland across the bubbling Blasket sound.

(4) On swinging around the first corner of the track, you are greeted with magnificent views over the Atlantic expanse. To the south, Iveragh's

Not only size helps in identifying birds, but also tail shape, wing position and colour markings. Left to right (beak to tail measurements): fulmar (18in), kittiwake (16in), storm petrel (6in).

peninsula reaches out into the dissolving mists towards the regal twin peaks of the Skellig rocks, home to many birds. Below you, the heath tumbles down to precipitous cliffs where KITTIWAKES kite over a rumbling surf, returning here to breed each summer after six months on the open sea.

(5) Having proceeded for several metres along the track, cut across the open moor at an angle to your RIGHT and make for the domed summit of the hill (764ft/254m).

The high road leads westwards to the elevated peaks ahead and the long, sloping spine of the island's topography becomes quite distinct, running out to sea for a distance of 4ml/6.5km. The islands are the unsubmerged peaks of coastal mountains drowned after the last Ice Age meltdown, and are really a continuation of the Dingle mountain chain. Their tough bony texture survives the onslaught of the sea because much of their base bedrock is made from ancient laval flows. Thus, the hard but steep-sloped hills run right out over the dizzy cliffs, with hardly a single bit of level ground discernible – a characteristic which caused the famous Irish botanist Robert Lloyd Praeger to remark that botanising on the Great Blasket was very like botanising on the steep roof of a church.

In early summer, the island shimmers green against a grey-blue sea. Later in the year, the swards of coloured HEATHERS smear the barren hills with shades of purple and pink, while the bright blue sky reflects in a turquoise sea.

(6) At the top of the hill, turn LEFT and continue to walk west along the island's spine. This leads to a ruined signal tower, though this is not yet visible.

Up here the wild and exposed scenery explains the paucity of vegetation on the island. The plants here are of a hardy nature and well suited to the maritime conditions. In the short grass will be found the SEA PLANTAIN (*Plantago maritima*) and SEA PINK/THRIFT (*Armeria maritima*). But the odd rarity, like the unusual-looking ADDER'S TONGUE (*Ophioglossum vulgatum*), also occurs. Small, and growing close to the ground, this plant is capable of handling Atlantic storms and survives in scattered pockets. Its only enemy now is the curious and naive tourist.

(7) From the signal tower, continue to walk in a STRAIGHT line westwards, making for the junction of the old roads visible ahead.

There is little of the tower left to see, as earlier this century it was struck by lightning. The tower, like many more on the mainland, was part of the coastal defense system put into operation by the British during the Napoleonic wars of the early nineteenth century. Just beyond the tower is a large square of heath marked out by flat stones. Inside this is another arrangement of stones, its outlined pattern more easily read from the air, and it would have been significant during the first transatlantic flights and possibly during World War II. With a little detective work you should be able to interpret the message!

(8) At the road junction, continue STRAIGHT, climbing the steep incline towards Doon fort.

This junction was known to the islanders as 'the traffic lights', even though the heaviest traffic here would have been a few donkeys carrying turf back from the high bogs.

(9) As you walk upwards, the road gradually fades into the thin heath. Before it disappears, watch for the outline of the fort above and on your right. Guarded by two defensive walls at its front and precipitous cliffs at its rear, it must have been a formidable retreat, though in all probability it was a sanctuary used during times of invasion and attack, rather than a dwelling site. Such promontory forts were a common feature of the ancient Celts and probably date from the Iron Age, about 800 BC.

(10) Leave the fort, rejoin the disappearing road and go to the RIGHT, continuing your journey west towards the summit of the nearby hill, Slievedonagh (937ft/300m).

All around you are excellent views. To the north is the barren island of Inishtooskert. Looking towards the mainland, the cliffed coastline of Kerry edges a land of rounded hills draped in expansive tracts of heath, their lower slopes covered in a tapestry of stone-walled farms. Visible in the distance are the lofty peaks of the Brandon mountain range, which dwarf the pointed peaks of the Three Sisters on the northern edge of the peninsula. To the right of the headland, the long ridge of Eagle Mountain overshadows Dromore Head, the most westerly point of the Irish mainland. Out to sea, the remaining members of the island archipelago are easily identified: on the right, the pointed pyramid of Tearaght bursts through the distant ocean, while out to your left, are the rocky and sheer-cliffed islands of Inishnabro and Inishvickillane, the covert of politician Charles Haughey.

(11) Leaving Slievedonagh, follow the path down the other side into the valley and head STRAIGHT for the highest point of the island, Croaghmore (961ft/300m) referred to locally as 'The Cró'.

Along the way, watch for the small stone enclosures called clochans. A perfect example is visible on your right behind Slievedonagh, perched above the plummeting cliffs. This has a small entrance door and projecting steps climbing up its outer wall, which is punctuated with a number of air holes. The islanders built these clochans for drying turf, which they stacked inside and then capped with a thatch of straw.

(12) Along the path, the rolling heath slides downward to thickets of bracken on your left, while the Fatal Cliffs drop down uncomfortably close on your right. Out to sea, sheets of white birds sweep across the ocean surf. GANNETS, like showers of white arrows, pierce the waves in search of fish, while across the choppy water surface, bobbing black rafts of small rounded shapes separate into AUKS, GUILLEMOTS and RAZORBILLS. The islands are one of the most famous, if not the most important, sea-bird haunts in the country, with vast flocks of thousands returning each summer to breed on the inaccessible ledges. Although the Great Blasket itself is fairly sparsely populated, Inishvickillane supports enormous colonies of STORM PETRELS or 'MOTHER CAREY'S CHICKENS' (*Hydrobates pelagicus*), while Tearaght is home to upwards of fifty thousand individuals, a sizeable proportion of the world's population. Similarly, great numbers of PUFFIN (*Fratercula arctica*), RAZORBILL (*Alca torda*) and GUILLEMOT (*Uria aalge*), also occupy the many islands. Fortunately, access to these significant and substantial breeding sites is severely restricted, and it is hoped that this will protect them from the considerable damage that overenthusiastic, albeit naive, sightseers can inflict.

(13) On reaching The Cró, stunning vistas of the outlying island network are unveiled beyond the rolling heath. Below you and to the west are two stone forts, quietly hidden away in this forgotten corner of the world.

The trailing stems and erect pink flowers of the bog pimpernel are
more common to the West of Ireland than anywhere else.

(8) From the summit of The Cró, go back the way you came to 'the traffic
lights' and take the grassy road to the LEFT. This leads you around the
northern side of the island.

This stretch is ideal for casting off your shoes and walking barefoot, like
the many generations that walked this track before you. This sheltered side
of the island supports richer swards of vegetation, with a greater number of
wild flowers. The purple heads of SHEEP'S-BIT (*Jasione montana*) nod in
the August wind, while, from June onwards, the damp and seeping
embankment on the right of the road is covered in the trailing strands of the
delicate pink-flowered BOG PIMPERNEL (*Anagallis tenella*), a plant that is
abundant and mostly confined to the west of Ireland. Above you on the
steep slopes to the right, a further collection of stone clochans is built into
the hillside, placed so as to take advantage of the sheltered conditions.

(14) Halfway along the road, the heath runs sharply down and over the
sheer cliffs. This is known as the Sorrowful Slope, for at the bottom of
these cliffs several of the island's fishermen lost their lives in the last
century. An unexpected storm blew up, smashing their fragile canvas
boats, or curraghs, against the cliffs. Fourteen of the fishermen drowned,
while their womenfolk watched helplessly from the place where you now
stand.

(15) When you reach the final bend that brings you back to the village
farms, leave the road and go STRAIGHT, down across the earthen-walled
fields, making for the beach called An Trá Bán ('the white strand'). The
island of Beginish, formed over four hundred million years ago from
volcanic ash, stands in front of you.

Beneath your feet, the white daisies of spring carpet the lawn-like fields. When summer approaches, the common MEADOW BUTTERCUP dominates, turning the earthen walls to gold. Little else prevails, the wildflower population having been decimated by the persistent foraging of SHEEP.

(16) Access to the beach is not easy as there is only one negotiable entry and exit point. Nearer the LEFT-HAND side of the beach, you should be able to scramble down the rocks onto the strand itself. You may have to search a little if you are unfamiliar with the spot, but persistence brings its own reward.

Not only is it a fabulous beach with marvellous views of the Kerry coastline, but it is probably the cleanest beach in Ireland. Due to the scant number of tourists, the usual plethora of plastic rubbish is completely absent. Though used by some as a place to swim in the summer heat, the water is bitterly cold. This is due to the strong currents that race through the sound, which resulted in a Spanish ship, the *Santa Maria de la Rosa*, sinking off Dunmore Head in 1588. However, this does not deter the many seals that can be seen swimming and diving offshore.

(17) Leaving the beach by the same access point, keep an eye on the time while you explore the village before catching the ferry back to the mainland.

Though rather ungainly on land, seals love to relax, either by basking on sea-shore rocks or floating with their heads poking out of the water.

17 – Mount Eagle

THE WESTERNMOST EXTREMITY of Ireland is at the tip of the Dingle peninsula in the ancient parishes of Corca Dhuibhne. Here, Mount Eagle sits perched above the sea, peering out across the vast Atlantic Ocean, like a watchtower standing guard over the western coastline. Hemmed in by the cliffs of Slea Head, it looks down upon the archipelago of the Blasket Islands and also commands excellent views of the peninsular coastline running in towards Dingle town. Scattered around the foot of Mount Eagle are the present and past remains of a large cross-section of the civilisations that lived beneath the shadow of the mountain. The old routes of the ancient Celts wander around its base and archaeological monuments lie scattered about the fields – the multitude of buildings which former dwellers inhabited, ranging from Iron Age stone forts to early Christian clochans or beehive huts.

Despite the long history of humans on the landscape of the peninsula, there is still something wild about its character. Whether it is the presence of the sea, the undulating smooth-domed hills, or the unfeigned and sincere friendliness of its rural communities, there is an enchantment about Corca Dhuibhne that is hard to ignore. How long this charm will survive, however, is hard to say. Dingle, like so many other places, is rapidly falling victim to the sleazy ugliness of blatant commercial tourism. Only on foot amongst the hills can the spirit of its ancient culture, its true inhabitants and its wild landscape, still be fully appreciated.

WALK DESCRIPTION

LOCATION: Start at Kildurrihy village. Travel from the small village of Ventry on the Slea Head road for 1ml/1.6km and take the first RIGHT by the shop opposite the church. Take the next LEFT at a crossroads. Then, take the next RIGHT at a T-junction which heads into the picturesque group of houses and stone buildings that is Kildurrihy. Turn LEFT up to the top of the village, where a track leads to the TV mast. Park by the houses at the bottom of the track.

TERRAIN: A tough cross-country trek over high mountain heath (1696ft/520m), along overgrown green-roads and quiet country lanes. It is rough underfoot, with some very muddy patches, requiring stamina, and is not really suitable for first-time walkers or very young children.

FEATURES: Mount Eagle and lake; boggy heath; Kerry Way; beehive huts; stone monuments; country lanes; panoramic views of the coastline.

LENGTH: 9ml/14.5km.

TIME: 5hrs.

EQUIPMENT: Strong waterproof boots with good grip and a knapsack for food.

WHEN TO WALK: Good at any time of the year, but quite stunning when there is clear sunshine and none of the haze that occurs during humid summers. Do not attempt the walk if there is a risk of low cloud or mist descending on the upper summit.

WALK OUTLINE

(1) Follow the track that runs STRAIGHT up the mountain from the village.

As you walk up the laneway, a large stone wall skirts the left-hand side. The individual stones are blotched white with paint-like smears of lichen. The grassy banks contain an extensive collection of wild flowers that changes with the season. In spring come the PRIMROSES (*Primula vulgaris*) and DAISIES (*Bellis perennis*), whereas the summer and early autumn throw out the yellow petals of SILVERWEED (*Potentilla*), HAWKWEED (*Hieracium*) and TREFOIL (*Trifolium*). You may also find the small yellow blooms of BLACK MEDICK (*Medicago lupulina*), the most symbolic of all Irish plants, as it is the most common source of shamrock worn on St Patrick's Day.

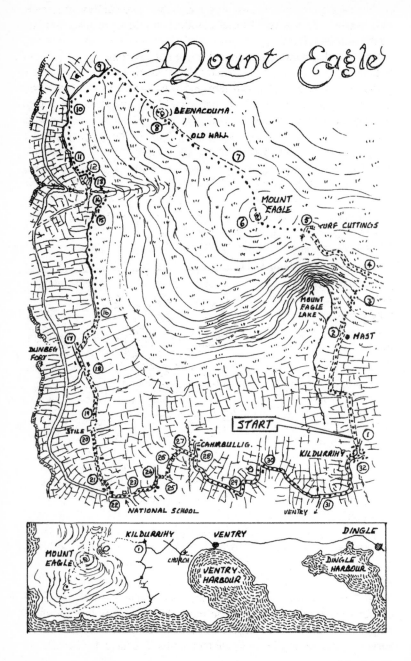

(2) Having passed the TV mast on your right, you eventually reach a gate. Pass through, reclosing it, and head STRAIGHT for the zigzag path winding up the mountain face.

Very shortly, the waters of Mount Eagle Lake become visible on your left, locked in the jaws of the cliffed sides of the mountain. The lake is a perfect example of a glaciated tarn and was formed by the last Kerry glaciation period. As you climb, better and better views of the domed heathered hills that ring Dingle and Ventry spread out behind you. Free from the scourge of coniferous plantation, much of the Dingle peninsula retains its original open heath together with its rich wildlife. It is possible that the forests that occupied Ireland in former times were never substantial in this windswept coastal peninsula. Indeed, it is quite probable that this is one of the reasons why Corca Dhuibhne is dripping with the artifacts of the earliest Celtic civilisations, as the dense, forested and swampy interior would have been full of BEAR, BOAR and WOLF, and so less easily inhabited by later settlers.

(3) Arriving at the top of the hill, keep going STRAIGHT until a bog road is met.

As you cross the boggier flat heath, pools of SPHAGNUM MOSS squelch underfoot, while RUSHES and tufts of HEATHER provide perches for a multitude of small moths, which rise as you approach. Keep your eyes peeled for the spectacular EMPEROR MOTH (*Saturnia pavonia*), a first cousin of the largest moths in the world. The emperor is brownish in colour and has

The emperor moth can look quite frightening when first observed, but it is totally harmless and feeds mostly on heather.

magnificent eye-spots on its fore- and hind-wings. Usually, its larval cocoon of silk, which is brown and incredibly tough and waterproof, is suspended in the branches of heather. This gives it every opportunity to survive unseen during the harsh winter months. The larva that hatches out during April and May is even more spectacular, being as large as your forefinger, bright green and encircled with black rings that are studded with yellow jewel-like tufts of spiky hairs.

(4) On reaching the bog road, swing to the LEFT and follow it to its end as it climbs towards the summit of Mount Eagle.

From the old road, you should now have panoramic views of the distant Blasket Islands. Stretching into the Atlantic mists, they are a photographer's delight on a clear sunny day. From the right, they are: Inishtooskert, stretched out like a corpse lying in state, hence the local name An Fear Marbh ('the dead man'), An Blascead Mór ('the Great Blasket') with behind it the pyramidal pinnacle of Tearaght, then Inishnabro, partly obscured from view, and finally Inishvickillane.

(5) The road ends before reaching the peak, so keep going STRAIGHT across the cut turf banks, and up to the summit marked by a concrete pillar.

As you walk, SNIPE dart from underfoot and shoot across the bog to disappear in other hollows, while the ever-present SKYLARK takes to the air high above your head and sings incessantly on the wing.

(6) From the summit, continue down the other side, working your way towards the next lower peak, which is at an angle to your RIGHT. This lies to the southwest and is best approached by walking first towards the Blasket Islands and then swinging left to follow the line of an old parish boundary wall, which leads to the summit of the lower peak, Beenacouma.

Having arrived at the summit (1696ft/514m), you are in the perfect place to take a break. Mount Eagle is the last mountain in the chain of peaks that forms the spine of the Dingle peninsula. It gives wondrous views over the magical mix of mountain heath, pristine sea and mist-shrouded island wilderness, that stretches out from you in all directions. If you sit silently in the warm haze of late summer or early autumn, the drone of bees will be heard clearly across the HEATHER. Lower yourself to the ground and skim your eyes across the top of the stunted heath and you will be amazed at the number of these honey-collecting insects screaming across the moor like a stampeding squadron of bomber jets.

(7) On a fine winter's day, the clarity of the air gives seemingly endless views across the horizon. You should be able to pick out the pinnacled shapes of the Skellig rocks far to the south, jutting out from the neighbouring Iveragh peninsula. While walking across the rather exposed coastal heath, there is a good chance you may spot some of the many migrant species that pass at various times of the year. In spring, numerous butterflies, such as PAINTED LADIES and RED ADMIRALS, wing their way in from the continent if the weather is favourable. Come the autumn, large flocks of swallows leave the coast to head down across the Bay of Biscay, and a variety of foreign species stops off for a rest, such as my favourite, the incredible zebra-striped HOOPOE *(Upupa epops)*. And if you are really in luck you may see the October-migrating WHALES going south to the warmer waters of the equatorial regions, where they will later give birth to their young.

(8) On reaching Beenacouma the way proceeds STRAIGHT down, following the line of the old boundary wall. It is a rock-strewn descent, so take time and care.

At the rocky summit of Beenacouma, a sheepfold nestles like a crow's nest above the panorama below. In the early part of autumn, the lawns of dwarfed LING heather come into bloom, spreading out in sheets of purple and pink. About the same time, RED ANTS *(Myrmica rubra)* are taking to the wing as they mate. These fascinating creatures herd small aphids and milk them like we do cows. On the way down, several small stone ruins are visible, but these are nothing more than sheep shelters. Below to the right, the hump of Dunmore Head encloses the romantic pocket beach of Coumeenole, a favourite spot with tourists in the hot summer season. It featured in the film *Ryan's Daughter.*

(9) When a large stone wall crosses your path, do not climb over it, but turn LEFT and follow the stony incline downwards. As you descend, you may notice a roofless clochan, or beehive hut, over the wall and across the heath. You will encounter better examples further on.

(10) Eventually, you reach another stone wall with some houses a little way down from it. Turn LEFT here and follow the wall east.

You have now joined the Kerry Way, a long route that rings the Dingle peninsula. Here, the vegetation of the sparse meadows is predominantly composed of DWARF GORSE. Between the GORSE clumps lie small patches of grass which attract the rare CHOUGHS, those red-beaked and red-legged black crows which come down to feed on insect larvae in the stunted grass.

(11) At the point where a wire fence meets the stone wall, you will encounter a black walking man pole. Go up to the LEFT keeping a stone wall on your right, until you locate a second pole.

(12) From the second pole go at forty-five degrees to your RIGHT to locate a third pole by the stone wall. You will have to completely circumnavigate the stone wall-enclosed fields on your right , which contain some cottages and stone clochans.

These clochans are NOT accessible. They are in a good state of preservation, as their domed roofs are covered in a grassy mantle. Many of them date from the Early Christian period, over a thousand years ago. They are commonly called 'beehive huts' because they are built in the shape of old-fashioned beehives.

(13) From the third pole follow the sheep track DOWN to the small Glenfahan stream.

This tumbles down from the boggy heath above. In mid-summer, lazy DAMSELFLIES flutter about its banks, although the stream generally has little wildlife due to its short journey to the sea.

(14) Having crossed the stream, the path rises up the hill at an angle to the RIGHT. Work your way up the hill through the short heath and locate another Way marker pole by the stone wall down to your right.

The stone walls are covered in a variety of lichens which means they were built a long time ago. The presence of lichens also indicates that the air is very clean as they cannot tolerate pollution.

(15) Having reached the pole by the wall continue to follow the line of the lichen-covered stone wall for the next 0.5ml/0.8km.

Above you on your left, the open hills of FURZE and heath stretch upwards and resound with the bleating of SHEEP. As you wander back along the heath, keep your eyes open for the various tracks and signs of different species. FOXES (*Vulpes vulpes*), for example, leave their whitish hair-matted droppings on exposed rocks.

(16) Eventually, you arrive at another Way marker pole by a metal gate that points down to the RIGHT onto another green road.

This tumbles down, rough and weather-torn, and is flanked by a stone wall to the right and a vegetation-smothered stream on the left. Further down, you may have to pass under a pole stretched across the laneway. This wild and overgrown laneway is sheltered by high walls and so draws the summer's crop of MEADOW BROWN (*Maniola jurtina*) and GATEKEEPER (*Pyronia tithonus*) butterflies to flutter about the BRIAR, mauve SHEEP'S BIT and PURPLE HEATHER, in search of nectar-laden flowers. On your left, the small stream gurgles amidst the choking stands of MEADOW SWEET and ANGELICA.

(17) Soon, you exit from the lane by a cottage and come out onto a tarred road, where you swing LEFT by a Way marker pole.

Pass a number of other houses with luxuriant FUCHSIA foliage, drawing swarms of BEES, WASPS and HOVER FLIES during August. Below you, to the right and above the cliffs, is the Dunbeg promontory fort, which may date from the Iron Age almost 2500 years ago. Overhanging the cliffs and cut off from the land by high stone walls, the fort was part of the defenses used by our ancestors to stave off the marauding tribes that plundered along the western seaboard. (A short detour at (18) brings you down to the fort.)

(18) After several hundred metres, the road turns to the right, but keep going STRAIGHT up the FUCHSIA-smothered green-road where another Kerry Way marker points the way. (Here, a gate may block the way; if so, climb over it carefully.)

The track gradually climbs uphill and is, in parts, covered with great clumps of FUCHSIA that can drench you after a shower of rain. The more open stretches are full of wild vegetation in which nature remains relatively undisturbed, a

Introduced by man, the delightful lantern-shaped flowers of fuchsia are a great source of nectar to insects.

welcome nature bank that supports such disliked plants as THISTLE, NETTLE and BRIAR. But without the stinging nettle we would no longer see the stunningly coloured PEACOCK BUTTERFLY. When the larvae emerge, in June and July, they feed only on the leaves of this plant. Therefore, we should suffer these unpopular plants gladly.

(19) The green-road eventually comes to an end and has a rough stile with a Kerry Way marker, leading into a field. Cross the field at a forty-five degree angle to the RIGHT and go downhill. This will bring you to another stone wall, with a stile in the corner, flanked by two large boulders.

In mid-summer, the yellow RAGWORT (*Senecio jacobaea*) and purple KNAPWEEDS (*Centaurea nigra*) crowd the ditches and some of the fields. RAGWORT is dangerous to cattle and so farmers are required to keep it under control. However, it is also the larval food of the CINNABAR MOTH (*Tyria lacobaeae*), which is recognised during summer by the yellow-and-black striped 'football jersey' of the larva. On pupating, their characteristic dark red spotted forewings and red hindwings make them memorable. They are sometimes confused with the similarly dressed SIX-SPOTTED BURNET – but that prefers to feed on vetch.

(20) Cross the stile to rejoin the green-road and follow it STRAIGHT down.

The views inland open up again, and away to the left are the rounded slopes of Brandon Mountain, while straight ahead Ventry Bay and the cliffed coastline of Dingle Bay stretch out before you. Pass the old ruin on your left and continue down along the BRIAR-covered laneway where, in August, the ripe and sweetened blackberries are a delight to pick.

(21) Presently, you pass through an iron gate tied with rope. After closing the gate, follow the lane DOWN to its exit between two houses and out onto a tarred road. Watch the heavy summer traffic here, as tourists drive bumper-to-bumper to view the delights of the Dingle peninsula.

(22) Swing LEFT along the road for about 300ft/100m, passing the old national school called Scoil Chaitlín Naomhtha (1928). Immediately after this is an avenue to a house and a narrow tarred road on the left. You leave the Kerry Way here.

(23) Take the tarred roadway to the LEFT.

As you walk up the narrow road between hedges of FUCHSIA, you soon pass some old buildings with clochans to their right. Soon after the two facing gates, watch out for a very overgrown laneway on your RIGHT.

(24) Enter the laneway on the RIGHT, passing through an iron gate further up. The laneway in summer is smothered with the delightful orange of MONTBRETIA flowers and whites of MEADOW SWEET. Follow the lane STRAIGHT for about 300ft/100m until it comes to a rather unclear Y-junction with a rough gap into a field at the corner.

(25) Go to the LEFT, up the overgrown and now very narrow lane, ignoring the more open FUCHSIA-canopied lane on the right.

Further up, as you walk, the sheaves of BRACKEN and BRAMBLE pull at your hair, but I like the way nature reconquers all once humans withdraw, and you are sure to see a multitude of BUTTERFLIES and the unpopular BLUEBOTTLE FLIES that find shelter in this deep laneway.

(26) Further up the lane becomes very overgrown and will prove difficult in the early summer when the new growth of briar pours on to the narrow track. On reaching an iron gate open and reclose it after you and proceed to a T-junction with a pole and blue Way marker arrow.

(27) A few metres further on, the laneway arrives at a T-junction. Go to the

RIGHT and follow the winding lane east, until it eventually crosses a stream and exits onto a tarred road by some farmhouses in the village of Cahirbullig.

At the point where the lane exits onto the tarred road, a fine old ELDER BUSH (*Sambucus nigra*) grows by the corner of the wall on the left. Judging by the girth of its trunk, this bush is extremely old, possibly over a hundred years. During June and July, it droops its voluminous white blossoms over the lane, while its blackberry fruits appear in autumn.

(28) At the tarred road, go downhill to the RIGHT and walk for several hundred metres to arrive at a Y-junction.

Along the way, the flower-decked roadside passes through a kaleidoscope of colours between spring and autumn. In May, the large trumpet flowers of YELLOW

The tall yellow stands of the yellow flag or iris are very characteristic of wet ground and appear early in summer.

FLAG (*Iris pseudacorus*) herald your arrival, while in late summer the pinks of purple LOOSESTRIFE (*Lythrum salicaria*) light the way.

(29) On arriving at the Y-junction go to the LEFT and continue along the tarred road to the next Y-junction.

If you are walking in August or September, you will be astounded by the flood of colour that greets you on rounding the third bend. Here, a torrent of orange-flowered MONTBRETIA pours down the ditch on the left. These garden hybrids were introduced from South Africa and have run wild in the damp ditches around much of south-west Kerry.

(30) Turn RIGHT at the next Y-junction by the corner of a two-storey house.

(31) Turn LEFT at the next crossroads and proceed to the village of Kildurrihy.

This is full of delightful stone buildings, between which the narrow road squeezes its way. This enchanting cluster of farmhouses and beautiful stone outhouses is an artist's delight; some of them are quite old and are fine examples of the ancient craft of the now almost extinct stonemason. Indeed, there are signs of a very ancient settlement here, with Celtic artifacts scattered about the village. Where the gables of a cottage and a stone outhouse opposite it face each other like an entrance gate, are two stones. The second of these is on the right, hidden beneath the FUCHSIA hedge just behind the outhouse, and is inscribed with a cross. A little further on, on the right, is a large stone, or bullaun, with a number of cup marks on it as well as inscribed crosses. Many of these stones are believed to date from the Bronze Age, which was in full flower roughly four thousand years ago.

(**32**) After the bullaun, cross a small bridge and turn up to the LEFT to the parked car.

Thatched with straw and crafted in stone, many of the
buildings in the village of Kildurrihy
retain their unique charm.

18 – The Magharees

THERE ARE MANY DIFFERENT HABITATS on our coastline that are both stunningly beautiful and that support a rich assemblage of rare and varied wildlife. These range from pinnacled coastal islands, through precipitous cliffs, to marvellous stretches of golden beach. But of them all, none is more unique and accessible than the unpretentious sand dunes that occur haphazardly around our shores. Little of the long and indented coastline of Kerry is composed of these expanses of sand, as they require very specific combinations of current direction, shelter and land position for their formation. On the west coast, where Atlantic gales can reach speeds of 100mph and send spray rising up to a hundred metres, it is a wonder that such delicate systems could ever develop.

As these habitats are exposed and constantly shifting with the winds, the small communities of plants that develop on them are extremely versatile and specialised. Some plants unfurl their leaves only when it rains, others may take up to thirteen years to produce flowers and reseed themselves. In this way, the inhabitants of the dunes have adapted in order to survive. However, their adaptations mean they can no longer survive outside these unique and ever-shrinking environs.

Two prime sand-dune habitats exist on the Dingle peninsula – the Magharees on the north and Inch on the south. Both are under considerable threat from human encroachment, mostly due to a lack of understanding of the rarity and importance of the areas. Ultimately, their survival must not depend on a few knowledgeable intellectuals – they need the support of a determined and well-informed public, whose actions, based on collective responsibility, guarantee their survival for future generations.

WALK DESCRIPTION

LOCATION: The dunes and beaches of The Magharees are located on the nouthern side of the Dingle peninsula, on a spit protruding across the mouth of Tralee Bay. Pass through the village of Castlegregory and follow the Fahamore Road for 1.5ml/2.4km. Park at the public amenity site for Maherabeg Beach, on your RIGHT and opposite the second caravan park.

TERRAIN: A very casual circular walk along the beaches and around the headland of this large sandy spit. During low tides one can follow the line of the beaches. But when the tide is in use your commonsense and stay up on the grassy embankments and on the dunes. Additionally, be aware that higher tide levels will occur during the high spring tides, around March 21 and September 21, when you must stay off the beaches.

FEATURES: Coastal dunes; fine beaches; dune and seashore wildlife; large estuarine bird sanctuary; impressive views of mountains.

LENGTH: 5ml/8km.

TIME: 3hrs.

EQUIPMENT: Comfortable walking shoes, with a windproof jacket on blustery days. Binoculars are an advantage.

WHEN TO WALK: The beaches are very popular during the warmer summer months, so it is better to avoid busy holiday weekends. Midweek is better, and you can have the place to yourself during the spring, autumn or winter.

WALK OUTLINE

(1) From the car park, walk onto the beach and swing up to the LEFT and follow the shoreline out to the headland ahead of you.

Approximately 3ml/4.8km long, the spit separates Tralee Bay to the east from Brandon Bay to the west. This creates a very sheltered aspect for the many birds that tend to drop off here for a rest during their spring and autumn migrations. You are also sheltered on this the eastern side of the spit, from the wild Atlantic winds that have helped create this long expanse of dunes. If you are here during the spring or autumn keep your eyes open for passing migrants.

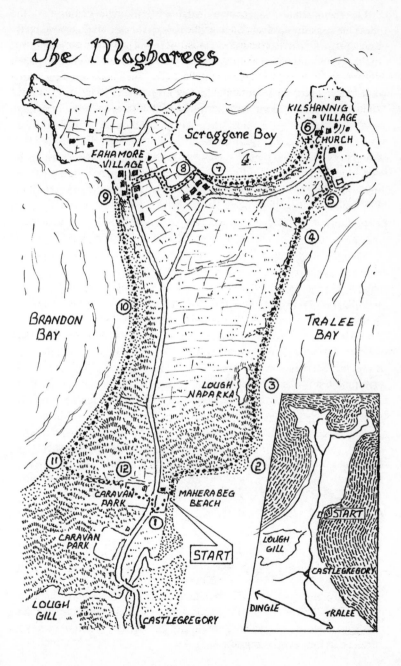

(2) On reaching the headland swing around it to the LEFT and continue to follow the coastline. Stay up high on the dunes if the tide is in, and even if it is out, as it makes for easier walking than long stretches of stoney beach.

The long expanse of beach may seem empty and monotonous, but much wildlife can be discovered here. Tossed up along the tidemark are the long, whip-like stems of KELP or OAR WEED, some of which can be 6ft/2m long. When these rot they, along with other marine debris, provide the breeding ground for numerous flies and SAND HOPPERS and thus attract birds like the RINGED PLOVERS (*Charadrius hiaticula*). Along the waterline, during the summer, you will undoubtedly discover stranded JELLYFISH which have been brought here by wind and warm currents. Generally harmless to humans, only a few, such as the rare PORTUGUESE MAN-O'-WAR and the LION'S MANE, can inflict a nasty sting.

(3) Presently you should pass the small, freshwater Lough Naparka on your left.

This swampy terrain, being rather inaccessible, is rich in bird life during summer and winter. It is a haunt of the GREY HERON (*Ardea Cinerea*) as it searches out aquatic prey and the place where a summer dweller and a rare amphibian, the NATTERJACK TOAD (*Bufo calamita*), another rarity of the southwest, may be found. This unusual Lusitanian species is more a native of the Mediterranean than Ireland and is found only in a few dune systems of Kerry. The toad is approximately 2.7in/7cm in length, yellow-greenish in colour, and has a warty skin. It is seldom seen, as it is generally nocturnal, but it makes a noisy racket during the mating season when it croaks all night by the freshwater pools. Sadly, the natterjack's territory is being encroached upon daily, as the dunes are seen as wasteful empty

places, ripe for exploitation, especially for golf courses. What the future of these wild places should be is debateable, but I think there is a strong argument for keeping them as they are – wild places to walk, explore and understand nature.

In Ireland, the natterjack toad is unique to Kerry, being confined to the diminishing sand-dune habitats.

(4) As you progress the dunes will have completely flattened out and reverted more to farmland. Ahead a number of houses are visible by the beach end.

On the grassy fields numerous wild flowers will be in full display in early summer, like the miniature BURNET ROSE (*Rosa Pimpinellifolia*) of coastal habitats. As you get further away from the impact of humans, the amount of bird life increases. The occasional group of OYSTER CATCHERS (*Haematopus ostralegus*) trots about the tide mark. These black and white birds have particularly long and pointed red beaks, which they use to probe the soft sands for the numerous invertebrates that live within it. Shelled bivalves, such as COCKLES, VENUS and RAZOR SHELLS, all have two shells around their bodies and live buried in these sands, extracting food by siphoning water through extended tubes. Another life form that is hard to see is the burrowing LUGWORM, though it forms a tell-tale coiled worm cast atop its burrow. Other worms do not burrow but are free-living – RAGWORMS, for instance, can grow to over 1ft/33cm in length and if handled improperly can impart a vicious bite. Watch your toes when swimming! However, it does not usually interfere with large animals and you would have to grasp one in your hand before it could bite you, nor is it generally found swimming so close to shore.

(5) On nearing the last white house by the beach, avoid any wet areas and swing LEFT onto the lane that leads up to the village of Killshannig. Note the ruined church on the LEFT of the cluster of houses and make towards this.

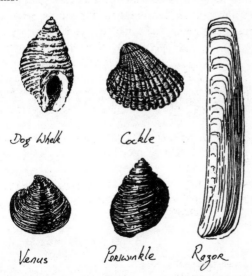

Dog Whelk

Cockle

Venus

Periwinkle

Razor

Many types of shell are found embedded in the sand and give a clue to the rich variety of species found in these unpolluted coastal waters.

During winter, the open sea normally has large flocks of birds on it. These are primarily COMMON SCOTER (*Melanitta nigra*), sea ducks that have travelled from the Arctic regions to overwinter in these shallow coastal waters. Dull black-brown in colour, they form large rafts on the surface of the water, at times numbering several thousands. The sandy bay suits their feeding habit – diving for the plentiful shellfish. Unfortunately, because of their need to live on open coastal waters, they are very vulnerable to oil pollution from shipwrecks. In summer, it is the white plummeting shapes of the diving GANNETS that catches your attention as they fly up from their colony on the Skellig rocks further to the south. The presence of such vast numbers of birds clearly points to the richness of these waters and the need for their protection.

(6) On arriving up by the LEFT-HAND side of the old church you should be able to scramble down on to the beach. (At high tide make your way up to the back of the dunes.) Cross the beach and make for the village on the other side.

This is Scraggane Bay, the haunt of a very different type of marine dweller – the windsurfer. At any time of the year if the wind is right, you will more than likely encounter these remarkable sportspeople shooting across the horseshoe-shaped bay. They have all the advantages of the wild coastal breezes without the choppy rollers that thunder outside the mouth of the bay. It is impressive to watch a group of experienced surfers cut across the bay at incredible speed, doing a handbrake turn with a flick of the sail and shooting back again.

(7) On reaching the end of the beach, watch for a walking man sign just by the roadside that leads up to the village. This points you on to the path atop the grassy embankment that runs above the beach and beside the fields at the rear of the houses.

If you feel you would like some refreshments, there is a shop and a pub about 164ft/50m up.

(8) About 328ft/100m further along the path, watch for another walking man sign on your LEFT that points you up a narrow laneway and through the surrounding small meadows. Follow the laneway up and around to a T-junction where you again go LEFT over to the village of Fahamore.

These fields are still very natural and in the warmer summer days the many wild flowers of the traditional hay meadow will abound, such as COMMON BUTTERCUP (*Rannunculus Acris*) and CLOVER (*Trifolium* Pratense).

Other coastal-loving species that prefer the more calcium-enriched soil also thrive here, for example the EARLY PURPLE ORCHID (*Orchis Mascula*), usually in flower between April and May.

With the flowers come the butterflies and on calmer days you should spot colourful TORTOISE SHELLS, PAINTED LADIES and the smaller COMMON BLUE as they flit about the nectar-laden blooms.

(9) On arriving out to a tarred road in the village of Fahamore go to the LEFT and shortly work your way onto the beach if the tide is out. (Follow the top of the gradually rising dune system if the tide is in.) Do NOT swim here – see point (11).

As you move along this beautiful stretch of beach there are some wonderful views across the bay to the distant Brandon mountain range as they plummet down to Brandon Head. The sheltered shallow waters of Brandon Bay cover an area of approximately 25,000 acres and are a very important wintering ground for thousands of DUCKS, GEESE and WADERS. If you are travelling here at any time from the month of October through to the following spring, you will delight at the vast flocks of BRENT GEESE, WIGEON, TEAL, MALLARD, PINTAIL and SHOVELER DUCK, as well as the countless numbers of waders, ranging from the very large CURLEW to the smaller TURNSTONES. This area is now a wildlife sanctuary and is a fully protected nature reserve.

(10) As you travel along the beach the sand dunes get higher and higher and it is possible to climb to the top. Narrow at first, they gradually widen, while away in the distance behind the highest of the dunes is hidden the large, freshwater Lough Gill. Here numerous types of waterfowl can be observed within the confines of the reserve.

Within the sheltered valleys of the dune slacks, several different plants are found. Some, such as BIRD'S-FOOT TREFOIL (*Lotus corniculatus*) and CLOVER (*Trifolium*), are very common; others are rarer, for example

Lady's tresses – easily missed, this small but beautiful orchid is now facing extinction because of threats to its vulnerable habitat.

the yellow SEASIDE PANSIES (*Viola curtisii*) and similarly coloured KIDNEY VETCH (*Anthyllis vulneraria*). Still others are in considerable danger of extinction in Ireland, both because of their limited distribution and threats from thoughtless individuals. One such plant is LADY'S TRESSES (*Spiranthes spiralis*), the most beautiful of all the plants that I have encountered – not just because of its rarity, but also because of the beauty of its frosted stem and leaves, which are topped by a spiral of white flowers. It is an orchid and so, like many of its type, has a drawn-out and complex life cycle, which, of course, increases its vulnerability. Some orchids have to wait thirteen years from the time one of its seeds germinates until it produces the flowers that will guarantee the future of the next generation of plants. Thus, to pick one of these rare blooms wipes out a whole generation and helps to give the plant that final push to extinction. It is hard to imagine that such an innocent act could cause such a significant loss, but I think this clearly illustrates the delicate and vulnerable nature of our dunes.

(11) Eventually the high dunes disappear about 1ml/1.6km further on and a large open space is reached on your LEFT. Follow this open breach in the dunes to the caravan park. There may be a sign here stating CAUTION: DANGEROUS CURRENTS. So do not be tempted to swim here but rather wait until you get back to the safer beach at the starting point of the walk.

The dune system here is not very highly populated due to the constant flow of people in and out of the breach. The resulting erosion means this part of the dunes is very unstable. From the top of the higher dunes, the waves of MARRAM GRASS (*Ammophila arenaria*) flow in a series of folds back towards the mainland. These valleys, or dune slacks, provide shelter and even accumulate fresh water, which gives rise to a different community of plants. On the more exposed hills, the dominant plant is the marram grass, its deeply penetrating roots holding the entire dune system together. It likes to get buried alive every so often, as this stimulates the growth of the smothered shoots which eventually form the massive network of root fibres holding the dunes together.

(12) On arriving up to the caravan park make your way out through it, using the rear stiles, and out onto the road. Cross the road to the car park and so to the starting point of the walk.

As you walk back from the beach you may spot a number of other coastal species about the grassy heath. Along the way, plants like the scarce SEA SPURGE (*Euphorbia paralias*), whose tall stem of fleshy leaves can retain water, are to be found.

19 – Kenmare Uplands

THE WILD UPLANDS OF KERRY can be inaccessible places, prone to extreme weather conditions, ranging from low temperatures and excessive wind exposure to persistently high rainfall. Furthermore, as very rocky and poorly drained areas, they tend to be wet throughout the year, and thus develop a characteristic type of habitat, namely the blanket bog. Here, only certain plants can survive and those that do thrive spread out in a suffocating soggy blanket that can dominate the entire landscape. As a consequence of this, both the density and the diversity of wildlife in these areas can be greatly reduced, and the habitat mistakenly looked upon as impoverished. However, nothing could be further from the truth as those organisms that have managed to eke out an existence have adapted in fascinating ways in their bid to survive. Additionally, the terrain of these unusual survivors is remarkable in its evolution.

In the mountains around Kenmare lay the centre of the last great glaciers to cover Ireland's southwest, the Midlandian ice sheet. This carved many fine glaciated valleys and overflow channels through the rocky terrain. Thousands of years later, these would eventually become the routes of commerce between isolated human settlements. Such old routes are now few and far between, but those that do exist grant a much easier access to the uplands, where the spectacle of real wilderness can be fully appreciated. Rumpled and buckled, fold after fold of mountainous heath undulates, while wave after wave of shimmering heather slides down, through and over rock-gullied cascade, splintering waterfall and shattered cliff – an uninhabited landscape, with neither sight nor sound of human presence.

WALK DESCRIPTION

LOCATION: The walk commences 2.5ml/4km from the town of Kenmare. Follow the side street behind Kenmare's central green, past the Catholic church. At the end of the town, take the first RIGHT turn at a Y-junction and continue in a STRAIGHT line for 2.5ml/4km, until you come to a T-junction. There is limited parking available here in the small layby, so please park sensibly.

TERRAIN: A spell-binding but very tough circular walk through the uplands, using two green-roads as access and exit routes. The section of trackless upland heath joining the two roads is quite strenuous. Thus, you need to be fit and agile, with plenty of experience. Definitely NOT suitable for casual walkers, or small children. DO NOT attempt it on your own.

OPTION: The beginning of the route from (1) to (11) is suitable as a moderately tough, oneway walk for the less experienced.

FEATURES: Upland flora and fauna; glacial features; blanket bog; mountain streams and waterfalls; aboriginal oak woods; old green-roads; abandoned settlements.

LENGTH: 8ml/13km. OPTION: 5ml/8km.

TIME: 6hrs. OPTION: 3hrs.

EQUIPMENT: Compass, and strong waterproof mountain boots or wellingtons with good grip essential. Knapsack for carrying food and suitable clothing. Irritating midges abound during the summer, so insect repellent is desirable.

WHEN TO WALK: A fine clear day is best in order to fully appreciate the extensive views and to be able to follow the route easily. To be avoided after excessive rain when mountain streams flood. Also, do not attempt this walk on days when there is a risk of low cloud, fog or mist.

WALK OUTLINE

(1) Arriving at the T-junction, go to the RIGHT along the tarred road.

If you walk along the old road during summer, the hedgerows will be wild and overgrown. Plenty of FERNS – BRACKEN, BUCKLER and LADY – line the old walls beneath a thin canopy of HAWTHORN, SALLY and

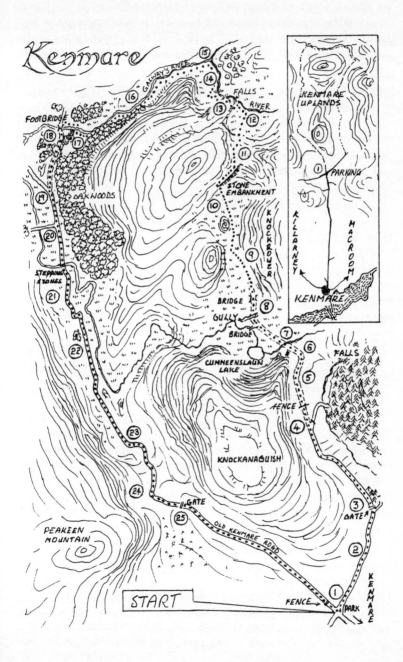

MOUNTAIN ASH trees. The south-facing hillside road is well sheltered from the north and traps any available sunshine, so you should catch glimpses of common butterflies, such as TORTOISE SHELLS (*Aglais urticae*) and SPECKLED WOODS (*Pararge aegeria*), that move about the brambles and wild flowers.

(2) Further on, the small fields of the farms run down into the shallow valley, where the rounded hillocks of numerous drumlins can be seen. These are the outwash remains of Ice Age glaciers that carved their way down from the upland valley ahead on the left. The ice has now been replaced by the sweeping swards of invading heath that pour down from the rocky uplands and encroach on the abandoned farmsteads.

(3) Presently the tarred road comes to an end at a Y-junction. Go to the LEFT through the forestry gate and follow the muddy track up by the conifer trees into the valley.

Across the valley, on the right, the high ridge of Coombane is cloaked in a thick coat of conifers. To the left of the woods the picturesque falls of the river Cleady echo across the valley as they cascade over the steep cliffed side. Recent development work indicates that these commercial woods are soon to be felled, so exert care if any trucks or machinery are encountered, giving them the right-of-way to carry out their work in a safe manner.

(4) On reaching another Y-junction in the lane, go to the LEFT, ignoring the better track with the gate on the right. Continue to follow the rougher green-road up the side of the valley, crossing over a low sheepwire fence that runs across the track ahead.

Up on the left, the black-cliffed rocks pepper the steep sides of Knockanaguish Mountain. Around the rocky terrain, discarded boulders are crowned with curious clumps of HEATHER and GORSE. Atop these lookout posts may be spotted some of the many STONECHATS that inhabit these hills, the dark head of the male being quite conspicuous. These small birds feed extensively on upland insects and are resident here throughout the year. Come the summer, the migrant WHEATEARS, with their distinctive black and white tail, arrive to compete with the stonechat for the mountain spoils.

(5) The track continues to climb UP the side of the valley and gradually becomes very wet and boggy. Along the way, the delicate white flowers of HEATH BEDSTRAW (*Galium saxatile*) may be found growing on the drier banks of the laneway, while MOSS and RUSH choke the wetter gullies. The heath bedstraw is a delicate cousin of the well-known GOOSE GRASS (*Galium aparine*), a plant whose hooked seeds you are probably familiar with. These small rounded seeds inevitably hitch a lift on your socks when you are out walking, using you to disperse themselves far afield. Not quite so successful in its adaptation to life on dry land is the moss. If you look carefully at the moss plants along the laneway, you may notice many thin-stemmed club shapes rising out of the wet green tufts. These are separate parasitic plants which

The delicate club-shaped spore heads that grow from the mossy tufts are an adaptation to aid spore dispersal by the water-dependent moss plant.

the moss tried to develop in order to live on dry land and spread its spores in the wind. However, this was a failure as it prevented the moss from reproducing – it has to revert back to the primitive water-dependent form to do so. The unfortunate moss now has to live a form of schizophrenic existence to survive – one part is water-dependent in order to reproduce, the other part acts as a parasite on the first, but is needed to aid spore dispersal.

(6) The track winds UP and around to the LEFT through an extensive scattering of crumpled rock and boulder.

On the left-hand side of the road is a dilapidated stone ruin which would once have been thatched. In pre-famine days, subsistence farmers, driven to the limits by tyrannical social conditions, must have found it nearly impossible to survive in such extreme locations.

(7) On reaching the top the track continues STRAIGHT ahead, crossing a stream that runs down from the small waterfall up on your right. If the stream is too deep, go to the LEFT, where it narrows, and jump across.

You have now entered into the southwestern extremity of Killarney's National Park. A flat expanse of blanket bog and wet heath stretches out to the circle of mountains, with the high peak of Knockrower to the right. On the left is Cummeenslaun Lake, a mountain tarn beneath the high cliffs of Knockanaguish and surrounded by fine stretches of wet heath, dominated by the lumpy tussocks of PURPLE MOOR GRASS (*Molinia caerulea*). This tall grass offers plenty of shelter, making it the perfect habitat for WOODCOCK and SNIPE, which feed on grubs and other insect larvae in the soft bog underneath. On fine sunny days, numerous DRAGONFLIES dart over the heath, having spent the long winter as larval nymphs at the bottom of the lake.

(8) Beyond the lake, the track rapidly deteriorates. A concrete bridge is visible on the left. Ignore it and continue STRAIGHT, but be extremely careful of the deep gully, full of water, ahead. This is several feet deep, but narrow enough to jump across. On the other side of the gully, the path swings to your RIGHT and crosses an inconspicuous stone bridge. For the next few kilometres, the route follows a STRAIGHT northerly direction.

The track is now little more than a footpath through the tall grassy heath, climbing up through a small valley of rocks interspersed with large hummocks of purple HEATHER. Walking through the tall grasses, you will occasionally come across large, fat, black hairy caterpillars with orange bands. These are the larvae of TIGER MOTHS (*Arctia caja*), which as adults are spectacular insects that usually fly at night. Their coloured wings are a marbled mosaic of white and brown with vibrant red underwings, which they flash at would-be predators to warn them of their poisonous nature.

(9) When the path tops the small rise, look STRAIGHT ahead in a northerly direction towards the distant rocky horizon. Head for this, 0.8ml/1km away. Continue downhill from the rise, cross a small stream and follow a poorly outlined path as it zigzags through the large tracts of swampy terrain ahead. As a general guide to direction, keep the high rocky slopes of Knockrower on your right until you climb over the distant ridge.

Beyond the stream and on the left is a fine stretch of bog, full of its characteristic plants. A sea of yellow BOG ASPHODELS (*Narthecium ossifragum*) coats the surface peat in late summer, while the white buds of COTTON GRASS (*Eriophorum vaginatum*) dominate in the earlier part of the season. Other plants are less spectacular to look at, but are fascinating in their adaptations. Such unusual examples as the insect-eating plants of SUNDEW (*Drosera rotundifolia*) and the GREAT BUTTERWORT (*Pinguicula grandifolia*) are found here in vast quantities, preying on the many insects of the bog for their source of nitrogen. A third, less familiar, insect-eater is the COMMON BLADDERWORT (*Utricularia vulgaris*), found in the wetter boggy pools. This carnivore of the bogs actually has little bladders, with attached trapdoors, scattered along its stem. The trapdoor springs open to suck in any passing insects which can then be digested. The yellow flowers of this innocent-looking plant poke above the bog water during the months of July and August.

(10) On nearing the high ridge ahead, you should notice the remains of an old stone road running upwards from left to right as you approach. Head towards the start of this by following the poorly defined path as it goes at an angle to the LEFT and use the old road as your route UP along the stony ridge.

The way ahead is wetter and has many waterlogged hollows. SPHAGNUM MOSS, SEDGES and various grasses grow profusely within these, and they are the main plants responsible for the blanket bog formation. As long as there is plenty of water, these plants will keep growing up and out to dominate everything else. Little oxygen enters the wet, smothered layers, which are laid down faster than they can decay, thus they gradually develop a very acidic nature that becomes intolerable to other plants. The grassy sedges are generally poor in nutrients and so are unattractive to the larger herbivores, but quite sufficient for the swarms of insects that develop in the muddy

The common lizard appears to be a formidable creature at first sight, but they are harmless and prey on insects. They will be more likely to skuttle off into the undergrowth in total horror at your presence.

layers at their roots. Some, like the CRANEFLIES, can emerge in such large numbers in favourable years that it would not be uncommon to find great flocks of SWALLOWS darting about the moors, feeding on the bumper crop of insects.

(11) The OPTION ends here at the top of the ridge. If you do intend to do this only, simply turn around and return by the same route.

NOTE: From here on, the route becomes difficult and extremely demanding, as it crosses over wet and slippery rocky ledges. There is no obvious path, and you have to follow the course of a cascading river down through wild and swampy heath – if the river is in flood this can be quite tortuous. Therefore, do NOT attempt to continue if you are inexperienced or ill-equipped. Return instead to the start.

OPTION

On reaching the top of the flat ridge (1200ft/370m), continue STRAIGHT, maintaining the northerly compass direction. On the other side of the ridge, follow the very rough outline of the old track down the other side, until the Galways River is met.

From the top of the ridge, the views into the distant uplands are quite overwhelming, and all I can say is, 'Welcome to the wilderness'. A rumbling buckled blanket of heath stretches across the entire landscape to soar up the sides of the mountains. Raw rocks rip through the thin peat in a series of ruptured and valleyed folds to splatter the sheets of heath with blotches of grey, white and black. Overhead, RAVENS soar, their hollow croaking echoing back from the surrounding hills. To the left is the peaked dome of Torc Mountain, while to the right is the higher summit of Mangerton. The latter is what is known as a nunatak, a peak that projected above the ice sheets of the last glacial period and so does not have the same worn-down appearance as those that were covered by the glaciers.

(12) On reaching the Galways River go to the LEFT and follow it along the riverbank down over the rocky terrain, maintaining a westerly compass direction. In general, when a steep ledge is encountered, go to its left and work your way down around it.

Ahead lies a land of innumerable waterfalls that spill down over the blackened rocks. Beneath the falls, deep crystalline pools mirror the enclosing cliffed ridge. Along the way, you may spot the familiar spotted KERRY SLUG which wanders over the wet rocks.

(13) The third waterfall reached is the impressive Poulagower Falls, where the water spills out over a broad flat sheet of rock in which it has carved many steps. Make your way with care down through the rocky ledges that skirt the falls.

As you scramble over the heather-clad rocks, the odd LIZARD may be seen scurrying into the surrounding vegetation. Ireland's only reptile, they spend the winter months in hibernation as they are unable to control their body temperature. Their cold-bloodedness also accounts for their regular appearances on sunny rocks in the early morning sunshine, while they wait for their body temperature to increase to allow them to begin the day's activities.

(14) Below the falls, thick tussocks of MOOR GRASS choke the more level riverbank and make progress slow and cumbersome. In the exposed heath, the variety of bird species is generally reduced. However, amongst the grass and sedges the occasional SNIPE may burst out from underfoot, and disappear across the heath as suddenly as it appeared. In the denser regions of heather, the rarer RED GROUSE (*Lagopus l. hibernicus*) can be heard issuing its characteristic *kok kok-ok-ok-ok* sound. Don't forget to watch overhead for the elusive HEN HARRIER (*Circus cyaneus*); the beautiful white-winged male is easier to distinguish than the dull brown-coloured female. During crisp clear winter weather, you may spot an unusual visitor to these mountains – the SNOW BUNTING, with its buff brown body and white underparts.

Damselflies can perform unusual acrobatics when they clasp together in the tandem position. This allows the female (rear) to bring her ovipositor in contact with the male genitals (front).

(15) Further down, the river levels out and is joined by a smaller stream to form deep slow-moving channels. Along the riverbanks, watch for the COMMON BLUE DAMSELFLIES (*Enallagma cyathigerum*) that appear from May onwards. If you are very diligent, you may even discover the empty larval exoskeletons, from which the winged adult emerged, attached to the waterside vegetation.

(16) Eventually, the upper treeline is reached. Trees grow up to an altitude of 1000ft/300m in the mountains of Killarney, an unusual characteristic in itself. These trees are part of Killarney's aboriginal OAK woods, which also contain SILVER BIRCH, HOLLY and MOUNTAIN ASH. The ground layer is covered in rich growths of mossy tufts, through which protrude FROTHEN, WOOD RUSH and SORREL. In parts, clumps of the delicate white-flowered WOOD SORREL (*Oxalis acetocella*) and ST PATRICK'S CABBAGE (*Saxifraga spatularis*) encircle the trees, which are themselves draped in sheets of thriving moss. The occasional dead tree is encountered, and these create equally important micro-habitats for the numerous decomposer species of the woods. Many of these are unseen, though the conspicuous BRACKET FUNGI projects from the decaying stumps like white plates. These saprophytic fungi are very host-specific and the species of a dead tree can be identified by the type of fungus that lives upon it.

(17) Follow the wooded riverbank downwards, eventually passing through some RHODODENDRON cleared woodland. Pass through and continue on down to a footbridge across the river.

As you proceed through the woods, they begin to yield their virginal wilderness to the scourge of the invading RHODODENDRONS. This introduced species now spreads so rapidly that in time it will choke the woods to death. Thankfully, through the voluntary work of young people and the OPW, this is now being cleared. The deep pools of water in the river may produce a rarity of these parts, the seldom-seen EMERALD DRAGONFLY (*Cordulia aenea*), which is found only in the upland heaths of the Killarney wilderness.

(**18**) Shortly afterwards a footbridge is met on your RIGHT. Do not cross but follow the better-defined path through the woods on your LEFT.

You are now back on another green-road, the Old Kenmare Road, part of the Kerry Way, which will lead you safely home. The rich OAK woods about here are partly cleared of the RHODODENDRON infestation and will gradually allow the natural regeneration of the woods to take place.

(**19**) The path leads out of the woods and across the edge of a bog onto a tarred road. Go to the LEFT.

A look across the boggy heath shows it to be full of the pine-scented BOG MYRTLE (*Myrica gale*), a plant that is more closely associated with the west of Ireland than the east. Along the roadside, boggy pools fringed in REED are full of croaking FROGS during the mating season. This occurs early in February, the resultant frogspawn heralding the first signs of an approaching spring.

(**20**) At a Y-junction, go to the LEFT. Soon, the road reverts to a stony track and you have to cross a stream that runs over it. This can be done by using the large boulders on the right that form a safe stepped crossing.

(**21**) As you walk along the old road, good views of the distant Killarney region fall away behind you, the woods and enclosing mountains blocking out all views of the lakes. The more open valley in these parts may provide you with the opportunity to spot soaring PEREGRINE FALCONS (*Falco peregrinus*), swooping down from cliffed eyries and kiting over the moors to flush out the flocks of smaller birds upon which they prey. Their nests are always atop high, inaccessible cliffs, so that their young are relatively free from danger. Thankfully, the numbers of this endangered predator are beginning to increase following their near extinction in the sixties from highly toxic pesticides that become lethal on entering the food chains.

(**22**) Further on, where the track passes near a river, a cluster of trees hides abandoned stone ruins on your right, a reminder of the evictions that were inflicted all along the Old Kenmare Road by nineteenth-century landlords who wanted to retain the whole area for their hunting expeditions.

(23) Pushing onwards, the track rises upwards, becoming greatly weathered by the many streams that run out of the surrounding boggy terrain. Rough underfoot, the route hinders four-wheel vehicles, but scrambler bikes are beginning to make assaults onto these fragile mountain tracks. Unable to tolerate this type of pressure, the tracks become slashed into deep muddy quagmires that eventually make walking on them a difficult and uncomfortable exercise, quite apart from the unwelcome intrusion these noisy machines make on the peace and tranquility of these wonderful environs. It would, therefore, be a welcome decision if the park authorities were to put some form of barrier at the entrances to these old green-roads.

(24) The track eventually reaches the top of the ridge and the valley on the other side opens up, with views of the extensive hills and dales of rock and moor running away into the distance. On the right is the high point of Peakeen Mountain, while to the left is the rugged Knockanaguish. Below, the flat expanse of moorland has been freshly planted with young conifers, the many straight drainage canals being quite noticeable. Their presence here will ultimately change the face of the landscape and remove the characteristics of the blanket bog, as well as masking the views of heath. It is argued that these plantations provide much-needed employment. However, rather then creating any worthwhile long-term employment for the residents of the area, these plantations generally benefit timber industries which are sited far from the source of the trees. Furthermore, the effect of this form of monoculture is to acidify the ground water, possibly causing a leaching of heavy metals from the soil. Thus, they seem to create more problems than they solve.

(25) On reaching a gate, go through it and follow the track to its very end. Rich carpets of sweet CHAMOMILE (*Anthemis nobilis*) cover the road, filling your nostrils with their aromatic scent during June and July. To the right, the waters of Kenmare Bay are visible, with the mountainous uplands of West Cork behind.

(1) Finally, the track reaches a wire fence with a footstile and leads you back down to the parked car.

20 – Barraboy Ridge

THE WILD, UNDULATING AND INDENTED COASTLINE of my beloved West Cork and South Kerry has the most dramatic mix of mountain and sea. Viewed from any of the surrounding peaks, the many sheltered bays and dividing peninsulas that comprise the region are always magical to observe and touch deep into the depths of your soul.

However, it is only when you climb to a reasonable height that one can fully appreciate the extent of the mountain masses and the enveloping sea. From Gougane Barra in the east to Dursey Island in the west, Beara's long, peninsular chain of rocky peaks runs out to sea for a distance of over 40ml/64km. North of this are the mountains of the Iveragh peninsula, while to the south are the rounded hills of the Shehy Mountains and the Sheep's Head peninsula. In between sit the wonderful bays of Bantry and Kenmare. Like a sheet of corrugated iron, the series of parallel mountain ridges and drowned valleys create a wilderness area that is of an ethereal kind. With roving mountain mists and sinking ocean sunsets, this place can be too beautiful to behold.

As a consequence of its strange topography, most of the area's farmland

and its many small towns and villages hang precariously on the edge, sandwiched between the deep blue sea and the bottom of the mountain slopes. The rest is pure, wild and abandoned, where I can wander for days lost to the charms of my beloved nature.

The route along the ridge of my adored Beara peninsula, which separates Bantry Bay from Kenmare Bay, is a classic walk and illustrates beautifully the fascination of this hillwalker's paradise.

WALK DESCRIPTION

LOCATION: Follow the N71 from Kenmare towards Glengarriff for 7ml/11.2km until you reach Bunane church on your RIGHT. Plenty of parking is available by the church.

TERRAIN: A strenuous, circular walk along a mountain ridge, using two old routes as access and exit. Suited to experienced hillwalkers who are proficient at map reading. Do not attempt alone or during low cloud, fog or coastal mist.

ASCENT: 519m.

LENGTH: 9ml/14.5km.

TIME: 7–8hrs.

EQUIPMENT: Hiking boots; approach shoes (optional); backpack, first-aid kit; walking stick; suitable clothing; refreshments.

MAP: OSI Discovery Series 1:50 000, Sheet No. 85: Cork/Kerry.

WHEN TO WALK: Only possible when there is no low cloud or fog on the hills. It can be tough after rain.

WALK OUTLINE

(1) Across the road from the car park of Bunane church, a quite side road leads down into the delightful valley of the Baureeragh River.

Sunk into the folds of the surrounding hills are several small valleys. With traditional farmsteads amidst crooked meadows, wooded copses and rich hedgerows, they hold the essence of what I love most about our disappearing nature. So charming and delightful, a remnant of traditional countryside survives, hidden from the claws of modern progress and Celtic hyenas. I want to walk up and down this stretch of country road again and again. Like all the rest, this too will be annihilated, it is only a matter of time. In the meantime, absorb, absorb, absorb.

(2) Having crossed over the sparkling waters of the Baurearagh River, a T-junction is reached. Here go to the RIGHT, following the tarred road for the next mile until you come to a distinct Y-junction with a walking sign.

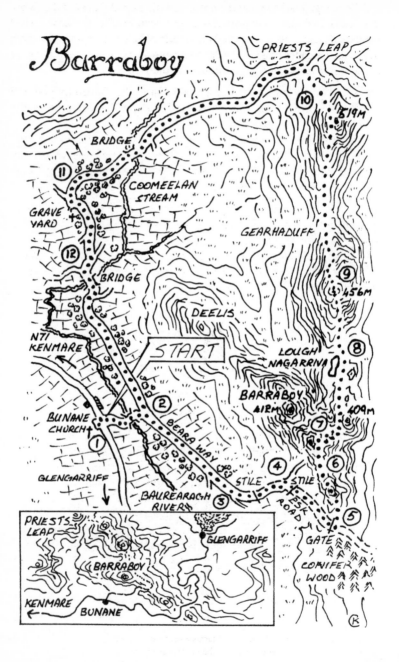

Barraboy

PRIESTS LEAP

10

519M

BRIDGE

11

COOMEELAN
STREAM

GRAVE
YARD

GEARHADUFF

12

BRIDGE

9

456M

DEELIS

N71
KENMARE

LOUGH
NAGARRIVA

8

START

BARRABOY
412M

409M

2

7

BUNANE
CHURCH

BEARA WAY

1

4

GLENGARRIFF

STILE

STILE

6

BAUREARAGH
RIVER

3

ESK
ROAD

5

GATE

PRIESTS
LEAP

GLENGARRIFF

CONIFER
WOOD

BARRABOY

KENMARE

BUNANE

R

A large signpost stands at the cross outlining the delights of the Beara Way, and it is along this route that you are now travelling. The narrow road winds and weaves its way around the small fields. SILVER BIRCH trees arch overhead, cascades of wild flowers pour from the hedgerows and all about the sound of birdsong echoes throughout the glens.

(3) A few tracks branch off into private houses, but hopefully you will arrive at the correct Y-junction where you follow the Way Marker up to the LEFT.

Presently, as the road rises, a gate with a stile by a small bridge is met. Having crossed, the road reverts to a stony track and leads out and UP onto more open heath land. This is the age-old Esk Road, and it is our access route to the ridge walk visible ahead.

(4) Later, another Y-junction is reached and the route goes to the RIGHT, crossing over another stile at a gate and following the steep and crumbling track as it leads you up onto the ridge top.

Looking back down, the delightful nature of the lower, virginal valleys is obvious, with those further to the east being the enchanting route which the homeward journey follows.

The old abandoned farmsteads give a romantic
atmosphere to the picturesque glens.

More often heard than seen, the cuckoo is a very distinctive
bird that bobs up and down when issuing its 'cuckoo'
sound through May and June.

(5) Having arrived at the ridge top, a coniferous plantation is encountered on the right. At the start of the plantation, pass through the gate and go immediately up the steep incline on your LEFT. Here you leave the Beara Way.

(6) Presently you reach the top of the ridge proper and the delights of Bantry Bay open up on your right, while down to the left is Kenmare Bay.

The route proceeds eastwards along the line of the Cork/Kerry border for the next 4ml/6.4km. In general you attempt to follow the summits of the ridge, rising and falling between the various high points. The heather-clad, rocky heath is tough in parts, so be careful of your footing.

(7) As you approach Barraboy Mountain, DO NOT follow the ridge line out to its 412m summit but swing to descend into the valley on your RIGHT, then work your way up onto the 409m summit. The descent is difficult and should be treated with care. Additionally, at the bottom there are deep swards of heather to be negotiated, thus be wary of hidden boulders and gullies. Looking east, you should be able to spot Lough Nagarriva, and you will be skirting this by its southern shore.

But first, having reached the summit of Barraboy Mountain, it is time to take a break and absorb the delights of the surrounding wilderness. Looking back west, the long spine of Beara's mountains dissolves into a clutter of peaks. On the left, Bantry Bay separates you from the Sheep's

Head peninsula, while on the right Kenmare Bay runs across to the lofty array of mountain pinnacles on the Iveragh peninsula.

God, what a sight, I could stay up here forever. Such scenes engender a great feeling of freedom and safety within me. It also gives me renewed hope when I think of the mass destruction of nature that is now taking place all over the Irish countryside at the hands of our new entrepreneurs and Celtic hyenas.

But they can't stop the river's roar
Nor the wave crashing onto the shore,
Neither can they wipe out a sunset's crimson glow
Nor the sparkle on the mountain of a winter snow.

(8) On reaching the placid waters of Lough Nagarriva, pass around its shoreline, keeping it on your left. Continue to rise UP and on towards the 456m summit. The most difficult of the terrain is now behind, other than a long stretch of undulating, mountain heath that has to be crossed before you arrive out onto the Priest's Leap road.

In places, unadulterated sheets of blanket bog encircle you with their delightful carpets of heathland flora, sedges and grasses. Beautifully intact, it is a delight to amaze the company when you plunge your hazel pole down several metres into the deep turf and explain the formation process involved.

(9) Having arrived at the 456m summit, you descend DOWN onto the saddle that separates the townlands of Gearhaduff on your left from Coumaclavig on your right. This is followed by a slow slog as you rise UP to the final summit at 519m.

Looking down to the right, Glengarriff Harbour, with its semi-tropical Garinish Island, is discernible. Down to the left, the exquisite wooded valley that makes up the homeward journey makes its appearance.

One of the earliest butterflies to appear is the orange tip butterfly, which emerges in April to coincide with the flowering of its favourite food plant, the lady's smock.

(10) Passing by the 519m summit the open heath eventually leads you out onto the Priest's Leap. There you follow the tarred road down to the LEFT and into the valley of the Coomeelan Stream, which you will cross twice.

(11) After a good two miles you are travelling through wooded countryside again. A side road appears on your right but proceed STRAIGHT ahead, passing down by the curious Garranes graveyard.

(12) Presently another road comes in on your left, but proceed on STRAIGHT to the next T-junction. Here go to the LEFT, cross over the Coomeelan Stream again and continue, through enchanting countryside, around the base of Barraboy Mountain and back to the T-junction of the outward route at point (2). Finally, going down to the RIGHT brings you back to base.